AF473105

What on Earth Are We Doing Here?

EXPLORING THE CASE FOR HUMAN SUFFERING

Elaine A. Piha

Balboa Press books may be ordered through booksellers or by contacting:

Balboa Press
A Division of Hay House
1663 Liberty Drive
Bloomington, IN 47403
www.balboapress.com
1-(877) 407-4847

ISBN: 978-1-4525-2979-0 (sc)
ISBN: 978-1-4525-2981-3 (hbk)
ISBN: 978-1-4525-2980-6 (e)

Library of Congress Control Number: 2010918086

Printed in the United States of America
Balboa Press rev. date: 03/09/2011

Contents

Introduction. vii

Chapter 1 The Intellectual Journey 1
Chapter 2 The Divine Design 17
Chapter 3 Interpretation is Everything 27
Chapter 4 Karmic Lessons 43
Chapter 5 The Gift of Suffering 57
Chapter 6 Understanding the Self. 73
Chapter 7 Accepting the Assignment 87
Chapter 8 The Invitation 95

Additional Quotes 97
Just a Few of the Books that Have Illuminated My Path. . . . 101

Introduction

Tonight, if you were to go out into your backyard, set up a telescope and point it toward the dark sky, at first, as you gazed through the lens, everything would appear blurry. The device would not yet be in complete focus or even be pointed in the desired direction. But then, as you carefully adjusted the dials, you would soon zero in on your target and the stars would come into clear view. The vast majority of us on Earth are on a similar spiritual quest. We search for clarity, for explanations, for answers, yet few of us ever take the time to properly adjust our dials. We remain content with the blurred view and therefore, many of us never realize the beauty of those distant stars.

I have always been drawn to stars, from the time of whimsical bedtime stories that included the midnight sky, to the gold foil stars we were awarded for good behavior in elementary school. Many of us were also lucky enough as children to enjoy the glow-in-the-dark solar sets that were plastered on our ceilings to resemble the outdoor sky. All of these were indirect actions that brought us closer to the magnificent mystery of nature. The night sky is full of wonder and each star represents beauty, mystery and imagination. Another magical component of nature is the starfish. This particular sea creature is fascinating because it can not only turn it's stomach inside out, but it also has the ability to re-grow a limb whenever the need arises, which is a sort of natural miracle. That same resilience, the ability to change and become the person you want to be, no matter what happened yesterday, is always within your reach. Life is about continually striving to be better than you used to be, rather than being better than anyone else. There is always a better you, your better self, just one good decision or one positive step away from you at all times.

We, as living beings, are influenced by the heavenly stars through our astrological signs, which sway our behavior and our personalities. We are also influenced by another type of star, the theoretical star of the media. The media is how most of us view and understand the world and Hollywood plays an integral role in this education and in how our society defines success, which on one hand appears to hinder our growth as a compassionate people, yet a closer look shows that the current media has embraced the supernatural and the metaphysical with more television coverage than ever. Under the principle of supply and demand, this increase demonstrates our escalating interest in such topics and the newly found exposure brings to light ideas and theories that have rarely been openly discussed, ideas that are helping raise awareness about the spirit world. This exposure has led many away from traditional religions and onto a path of spiritual exploration and self-discovery.

In terms of exploration, have you ever pondered your place in the continuum of life? Have you found yourself harboring a suspicion that there just might be more to life than you previously imagined? Something beyond the intrigue of reality television or the career ambition so widely revered? When one understands their role on Earth and their purpose in life, their confidence rises and we are all quite familiar with the liberating benefits of increased levels of confidence. As human beings living this spiritual experience, a common thread is our need for something to believe in, something that will provide hope. It is the human condition to have the desire to understand ourselves and our place in the universe. Plato, Greek philosopher, described man as "a being in search of meaning". Many of us begin this search through some form of exposure to organized religion where we often become familiarized with concepts like fear, guilt and damnation. Unfortunately, fear is what religions are often based on and what they rely on for compliance, yet fear clouds our thinking. Fear creeps into our minds like a fog and makes it difficult to see the road before us. As we become a more mobile, independent society, where people are less likely to accept another telling them what to do or how to think, religions are giving way to a more individualized approach. This approach moves us beyond religion and becomes a personalized journey that leads toward spiritual wisdom.

"God requires no synagogue except in the heart."

HASIDIC SAYING

The search for spirituality is as individual as our looks and there are an unlimited amount of paths that lead to the same destination. I wholeheartedly believe that human life has real purpose, a deep, meaningful, connected purpose and that there is perfection in everything around us. However, the understanding of that perfection, the meanings and energies of everything around us, requires a comprehensive evaluation of the actual experience of life, the spiritual experience we encounter during every single moment of our lives. What if I told you that you could discover a profound meaning for your own life? One that could not only make you feel completely empowered, but also thoroughly at peace and full of gratitude? One that would lead you to no longer fear death and no longer feel a sense of urgency about "living"? Through the pages of this book, you will discover how each individual takes on the massive responsibility of living a human life and living it with true meaning and purpose. Yet, in order to live with purpose, one must first understand that purpose and how it relates to their daily choices.

No matter where you have been or what you have experienced, some of the thoughts in this book will likely press you to re-think all that you have been told before today. You must maintain an open mind as you simply absorb all of the information. This openness will allow you to build your personal foundation and ultimately piece together your own truth as you journey to discover your true life's purpose. My motivation is to get you to open your eyes, but not to tell you what to see. When you come across a new thought, store it and continue exploring. Do not dismiss it nor devour it. It may take two or three reads to fully grasp, but keep going. I promise you, it will change your life!

Yes, challenge everything you believe, but remember there is a profound reason this book has found its way to you at this juncture in your life. This book is for those who have surpassed the limitations of religion and are ready for the next step of spiritual evolution. Spirituality is about your level of consciousness and the progression toward awareness. Humans are meant to evolve into conscious beings, yet we are often wicked in our mindlessness, thus, thinking without awareness is the ultimate human affliction.

Once you find your own truth, you will be rewarded with a peace unknown. You will no longer feel the need to pass judgment on yourself or others. You will no longer feel the need to live by other's rules. You will no longer harbor fear toward the mysterious and you will soon discover how valuable it is to live in the present.

"Believe nothing, no matter where you read it, or who said it, no matter if I said it, unless it agrees with your own reason and your own common sense."

BUDDHA

I was once, like most, down on my knees looking for answers, answers for the suffering and the devastation in our lives, answers for the destructive nature we have on each other and often on ourselves. Sam Keen, American philosopher, once said, "To be on a quest is nothing more or less than to become an asker of questions." Thankfully, my quest put me both on my knees and on my feet. This intensive search began nowhere else but within my own soul. We must all go within. We must all take responsibility for our choices and our actions because, after all, our current life situations are a direct reflection of all of our previous thoughts and intentions.

Again, the life you are living in this very moment is a mirror image of all of your collective thoughts, intentions and actions up to this point. Many people have a difficult time accepting this idea because it implies that they have played a role in their own misfortune, while actually having the power and control all along. Many want to believe that all of their afflictions are a direct result of someone else's actions, not their own. As humans, we are not typically strong at accepting responsibility, although we are well practiced at placing blame and fault. As you read the words of this book, the words will become thoughts and the thoughts will become actions. You will begin to think thoughts you have never imagined. The impetus is to inspire new expansive thoughts, feelings and beliefs and open a door for you that will never close. In a sense, just like the amazing starfish, you will discover a new resilience, a rebirth and an inevitable growth.

"As one person I cannot change the world but, if I change the world of one person, then my job is done."

Anonymous

Chapter 1

The Intellectual Journey

"I set out to learn what I most needed to learn."

THOMAS EDISON

Thomas Edison was the inventor of the light bulb. He was also afraid of the dark, which was the inspirational force behind his ingenious invention. His dilemma was similar to my own experience regarding organized religion. As a young child attending a mid-western Catholic school, I remember feeling as if I was being forced to live under some enormous dark cloud. The religious beliefs that were recited to me daily held no sense of belonging for me. I was unable to wrap my mind around what I was being told and I was unable to make sense of the anguish that religion brought to the lives of those around me. Church became an intimidating setting, a place filled with fear and doubt, rather than a place of joy, admiration and praise. I remember the looming thought that one lifetime was all we got, one short, unexplained, often miserable lifetime and it either lead directly to heaven or directly to hell. This was a very damaging way for a young child to view the world, a world that I later discovered holds so much beauty and so much joy.

I felt so out of place during those years and I held inside so many unanswered questions. What is the purpose of life? Why do humans inhabit this planet for such short periods of time without any explicit instructions or concrete guidelines? Why do we possess an innate drive to feel connected to each other, to nature and to the divine? Why do we suffer so much and love so little? Is there truly an afterlife? If so, what is it and is it our only chance for pure happiness? And, if true bliss is the ultimate goal, why then is happiness so elusive to us on Earth?

Happiness and a sense of purpose are synonymous and it is no mystery why we spend so much time and effort seeking either one. The search for happiness has been at the root of all human activity throughout the ages. Human behavior flows from three main sources: desire, emotion and knowledge. When you review the intention or motive behind most human action, the underlying desire is for one to be happy, or at peace. Curiously, we often begin this search for happiness outside of ourselves, from an external locus, rather than from within. One of the finest gifts you can give yourself, or anyone else, is peace and forgiveness. "When you are able to find peace within yourself, you become the kind of person who can live at peace with others," taught Mildred Lisette Norman, aka the Peace Pilgrim. You no longer feel the need to compare or judge yourself or others and you learn to value each person's contribution to the whole.

"You will have great difficulty achieving peace of mind and joy unless you respect how others choose to live their lives. That means respecting everyone's choices: the drug dealer on the street, the Pope, a homeless person, the president of the United States."

James Blanchard Cisneros

In our current society, we commonly derive our self-worth from what we do for a living or how much money we have in the bank, rather than from the good deeds we perform or the amount of love we share with others. Imagine if, instead of asking first, "What do you do?" upon meeting someone new, we traditionally asked, "What was the nicest thing you did today?" Our focus and perception of what is truly important may significantly change for the better. Achieving happiness, or a true sense of self, requires great patience, continual practice and keen personal awareness. Great diligence must be maintained while searching for and attempting to understand the elusive answers. Practice must become part of your everyday life, where you practice living your values, and finally, personal awareness is required in order to explore and fully understand your own actions and the role you play in creating the life unfolding before you. This joy, this purpose, comes from within and it lies inside each one of us, simply waiting for us to notice it.

The central goal of self-study is to discover why we are given the precious gift of life and what the reasons are behind everything that happens to us. Great confidence comes from understanding our purpose and this understanding allows us to move forward to live life without fear. Every single thing in this universe has a higher meaning. Everything speaks to us and, as I have grown in this awareness, I have learned to surrender to the magical, purposeful flow of life. I now see the perfection and the message in everything around me. I now see the brilliance in how each of our lives unfolds just as we have planned. I now see the divine order in all that I had previously questioned and I wish for this same trust to develop inside of you.

The question then becomes, "Who *really* has the power?" Life can often feel meaningless, cruel and unforgiving, but, what if I told you that <u>you</u> were responsible for every minor detail in your current life? That no higher source had solely selected this path for you, but that prior to birth you personally pre-determined the challenges you are experiencing and that you made a contract to live out that arrangement? That essentially, this contract was a blueprint for your life and an overall plan for the evolution of your soul? What if I told you that understanding this agreement could lead to boundless personal growth and freedom, including an understanding of why humans endure so much suffering? Acknowledging our blueprint is the difference between expecting God to handle the details and realizing we actually possess the power to design our own lives. What would be the point of human life if some higher source truly controlled it with puppet strings? The moment you realize that no one is going to rescue you is the moment you become empowered to rescue yourself.

Your choices in life, from the very first moment of genetic selection, have had purpose. They have been part of a larger plan, a plan that you created, for good reason. All of us as humans want to be in control of our lives. When we are not in control, we often feel powerless, victimized, even alienated.

When we are in control, we feel powerful, actualized and happy. There is great power in discovering your role in your own life. This discovery will allow you to exhibit greater personal command and learn to deal more constructively with the challenges that come your way.

We are all full of questions. We have all had the same hesitations. We have all wondered the same thoughts regarding our lives and, although I have always thoroughly enjoyed life, I still found myself frustrated that I was unable to place true meaning on the suffering I saw all around me. This same frustration is what initially spurred my research and later sparked my interest in sharing this knowledge with everyone that holds the same questions deep in their heart. Although I am now convinced that there is room for all belief systems and that no one religion or spiritual theory should reign sovereign, I was unwilling to simply accept what had been recited to me as a child for absolute truth and I encourage you to explore in the same fashion, to maintain an open mind, to re-think everything you have been trained to believe and to seek and to find your own truth. I encourage you to find a truth that comes from your heart, one that makes sense to you, both body and soul.

"Acquire the courage to believe in yourself. Many of the things that you have been taught were at one time the radical ideas of individuals who had the courage to believe what their own hearts and minds told them was true, rather than accept the common beliefs of their day."

Ching Ning Chu

My intensified studies began in a typical way, at the local bookstore, staring at the sea of books, all offering helpful advice on how to piece this mystery together. Throughout my quest, I was continually drawn to studies of past-life regressions, near-death experiences and the work of both mediums and psychics. Books would randomly appear from various sources, family, friends, colleagues, etc. I began to take notice of these beautiful coincidences and I placed significant meaning on their arrival in my life at the time because, after all, even Sigmund Freud, the father of psychology, did not believe that coincidences were without meaning. He also placed genuine meaning on such occurrences and believed that our conscious minds continuously recognize things that we were already aware of in our unconscious minds. I realized the universe was speaking to me and I knew enough to pay attention.

The more I read on these subjects, the more I wanted to read, and a few of the most cherished works included those of Sylvia Browne, Edgar Cayce, Dr. Raymond Moody, Dr. Michael Newton, Robert Schwartz and Dr. Brian Weiss. Amongst them, they have been involved in thousands of past-life regressions and near-death experience (NDE) recount sessions that provide insight into our life between lives, the time we spend in the spirit world. Alone, Edgar Cayce, one of the most widely publicized and meticulously documented psychics in history, was involved in over 2,500 life readings and over 14,000 physical readings, all of which he performed at no cost to the subject. His goal was simply to help others and he remained devoted to this compassion even through his own financial woes of the Great Depression. Cayce, the sleeping prophet, would use a simple self-hypnosis technique during his sessions as a stenographer recorded every word. While under hypnosis, with only an eighth grade education and no medical training, he was able to use specific medical terminology to prescribe treatments for his subjects, many of which had given up on finding a cure for their ailments. He was able to tap into cosmic energies and universal knowledge that he was not acquainted with during his waking life. The documentation of each of his recordings is currently archived and open for public review at the Association for Research and Enlightenment in Virginia Beach, Virginia.

Dr. Raymond Moody, author of Life after Life, coined the term "near-death experience" in 1975 during his research of more than 100 people who experienced clinical death and later recovered. He has since continued to pursue the phenomenon and the testimonies of his subjects, and countless others, have been so remarkably similar, as well as uplifting, that they have inspired many to change the way they view life, death and the hereafter. Following the frequently life-changing NDE, the emphatic message that survivors most often want to share with others is that there truly is an afterlife and that this glorious place is a place of total understanding, complete peace and absolute love. They often describe the sensation of traveling through a tunnel or of floating on a river toward a brilliant light source. Their vision of the afterlife does not include a vengeful deity, but instead a figure of complete love and compassion. Amazingly, many of them were non-believers before their experience and were later inspired to share their encounter and their newly-found knowledge with anyone willing to listen to their story. There have since been countless studies and books written on this topic, all of which report nearly identical experiences. One of the most recent books, Evidence of the Afterlife, written by Jeffrey Long, M.D. with Paul Perry, involves an in-depth study of over 1,300 people who have also had near-death experiences. This study included, not only adults, but also very young children who were not yet able to conceptualize death, yet their NDEs contained nearly identical content to the adult NDEs. This study also included several people that were blind at birth, yet were able to describe in great detail what their ethereal experience looked like aesthetically. The variance of ages and cultures in these countless studies, combined with the fact that they enjoyed extraordinarily similar experiences, makes it nearly impossible to ignore the conclusions and the existence of this magnificent afterlife.

The survivors' stories and the collective findings of the multiple psychics, mediums, clinical researchers and medical personnel clearly signify there is a true spirit world, one in which we still exist as what we know of as our inner-selves, our spirits, our souls. The very essence of our being is our soul, which is made up of electricity, a series of rapid and electrical impulses, just as is the universe. Everything around us has an electromagnetic field and is constantly vibrating. Every single object is composed of energy and that includes the galaxy, our planet and all living creatures. Even our thoughts and consciousness are vibrations. Sir Arthur Eddington and Sir James Jeans, two of the most prominent and accomplished astrophysicists of the 20th century, embraced the view that consciousness was likely the foundation of the universe itself and they stated that the universe looked more like a great thought than a great machine. Our spirits are nothing more than this same energy and pure energy cannot be destroyed; therefore, our spirits can never be destroyed. We are, in a sense, invincible. Plato wrote, "The soul of man is immortal and imperishable." We continue to exist beyond human life in a place commonly referred to as The Other Side, a place of indescribable beauty and peace. This spirit world is a place of unconditional love and extraordinary joy, where we are free to play, study, socialize, relax and create at will. It is a place where no judgment, nor time constraints, nor suffering exists. It is comprised of a beautiful landscape and spectacular buildings made of the finest materials, where we listen to beautiful music, enjoy the company of friends and appreciate the arts. Located here is the magnificent Hall of Records, where the Book of Lives can be found. This book contains an absolute record of our every thought, word and act. It is a complete collection of our entire earthly "experience". This book is also commonly referred to as the "Akashic Records" or the "Universal Memory of Nature". Akasha is a Sanskrit word that refers to the fundamental, or most basic, substance of the universe and upon this record remains an indelible impression of every movement, thought, and sound since the beginning of the universe. "The Akashic Record (also called the Akashic Chronicle) is the enduring record of all that happens, and has ever happened, in the whole of the universe," wrote Ervin Laszlo in his book Science and the Akashic Field, An Integral Theory of Everything. Akasha registers these impressions and the vibrations can be tuned into either naturally, for some, or with practice for others. The mere existence of this Book of Lives accounts for the ability of clairvoyants to literally *see* the past and that same ability lies within each of us. Edgar Cayce believed that the human mind is capable of processing a great deal more information than we are usually conscious of doing and therefore, he would put himself into a trance to tap into this universal knowledge that was already there, i.e., the Akashic Records. Here, he would gain understanding that was unavailable to him during his waking hours. He was able to make astoundingly accurate medical diagnoses, as well as view the past and predict future events while under hypnosis. This technique is quite similar to what we know of as meditation, a practice designed to quiet the mind and tap into a higher consciousness.

"For behold, this is my work and my glory – to bring to pass the immortality and eternal life of man."

MOSES 1:39

The thought of an afterlife or an eternity has been commonplace since the beginning of time, but today as the veil of consciousness is being lifted and our understanding of the spirit world continues to broaden, there is also an increased belief in reincarnation, the act of living multiple lives. A recent Gallup poll stated that three in four Americans believe in the paranormal and that at least one in four believes in reincarnation. These numbers are expected to continue to rise as the subject is further explored. Yet, despite the moderate western world numbers, the truth is that the majority of people in the world today believe in reincarnation, with the more traditional eastern philosophy followers leading the way. With most of the world believing in it, you are actually in the minority if you do not believe. "God generates beings, and sends them back over and over again, till they return to Him," Qur'an, Islam's holy book. Interestingly, there were references to reincarnation in both the Old and New Testaments of the Holy Bible but they were taken out for heresy, despite being accepted by early church leaders.

Understanding reincarnation also helps us understand the inequities in life. Through multiple incarnations we are able to experience whatever our souls wish to learn along the spectrum. We each have the opportunity to be rich or poor, to die early or to live long, to be healthy or to experience illness and so on. It is your individual self that chooses what you want to experience, not the Creator.

Reincarnation suggests that we have one eternal soul that never ceases to exist, but that this soul inhabits different human forms. Different bodies, same soul. There is a supportive saying by Pierre Teilhard de Chardin, French philosopher, that asserts, "We are not human beings having a spiritual experience, but rather we are spiritual beings having a human experience." This adage succinctly sums up the research by proclaiming that we are here on Earth to simply "experience". We come to the physical plane purely to experience life and love, not only for ourselves, but also for all of mankind and for the divine. "Life is just a chance to grow the soul," writes Powell Davies, minister of the All Souls Church, Unitarian. This <u>experience</u> is all there really is, our souls are eternal and the knowledge gained from each individual experience adds to the collective consciousness or the global soul. This collective consciousness is the knowledge base of the divine and holds the sum of all of the knowledge gained through each earthly experience. In the book, <u>Evidence of the Afterlife</u>, one of the subjects reported, "When I looked into his eyes all the secrets of the universe were revealed to me. I know how everything works because I looked into his eyes for a moment. All the secrets of the universe, all knowledge of all time, everything. I understood (I use this term because I did not actually hear) the colored drops were the experiences of all who had lived. The experiences existed as separate items yet belonged to the whole. The whole was the collective knowledge of all." Our task is to learn, to become God-like through knowledge and experience. Through this knowledge we approach our union with the Creator. Thus, we are all working together toward perfection and it is in our best interest to support one another as we move along this path.

In the search for the meaning of life, past life regressions are most valuable because they give us perspective on reincarnation and the process in which we move from one plane to the other. Questions were raised during these countless regression sessions and a consistent theme was discovered in the findings. The common conclusions were (1) that human suffering does have genuine purpose, (2) that human life truly is lived multiple times and, (3) that we choose our destiny prior to birth and then we write a detailed blueprint for that life to help us achieve that destiny. Robert Schwartz, Courageous Souls, refers to the development of this blueprint as pre-birth planning.

We all have within us a soul and this soul will continue to exist beyond our short time on Earth. We reincarnate and live multiple lives, but what would make a spirit want to leave the incomparable afterlife to return to Earth, a place of pain and suffering? Why would a soul want, or need, any further human experience beyond a single lifetime? Well, there is nothing haphazard about our existence. Albert Einstein, German-born physicist, agreed when he said, "I refuse to believe that God plays dice with the world." Nature does everything by intelligent design. The grass does not strain to grow, nor do we need to strain to live a life of purpose. Our lives have deep meaning. They are not unplanned or accidental. On The Other Side, between lives, we plan them. We create a detailed blueprint for the next lifetime and just as activities take place behind the scenes before a stage curtain goes up, preparations occur in the spirit world before each human is conceived. Once we decide to come to Earth, we create a plan for this life based on what we are most interested in experiencing and what we are most interested in learning to overcome in our eternal pursuit of knowledge.

"I could well imagine that I might have lived in former centuries and there encountered questions I was not yet able to answer; that I had to be born again because I had not fulfilled the task that was given to me."

CARL JUNG

Cultures from all over the world have ideals about how we develop this pre-birth agreement. Plotinus, Greek philosopher, wrote, "Each soul selects its body, parents, birthplace and circumstances of life. Then, as if a herald were summoning it, the soul comes down and goes into the appropriate body." Plato wrote, "A divine guide informs an assembly of souls ready for birth: 'No divine guardian shall draw lots for you, but you shall choose your own guardian and destiny.'" Rudolf Steiner, Swiss author, wrote, "The ego of the unborn and the spiritual hierarchies of the cosmos work hundreds of years preparing the spiritual blueprint for the developing body." Emily Dickinson, American poet, wrote, "The soul selects her own society, then shuts the door on her divine majority, obtrude no more." The belief in this cosmic design has been around for centuries, however, only now, in this current age of free-thought, has it become so prevalent in the western world. This New Thought Movement began to develop in the late 19th century and focuses on the effects of positive thinking, the law of attraction, creative visualization and personal power. It builds upon eastern beliefs and promotes the idea that all sickness, or suffering, originates in the mind and that "right-mindedness" or "right-thinking" has a healing effect. Yet, taking time to actually think in the western world is rare and often frowned upon in this high speed society. "To be mindful in the 21st century is to swim against the current," notes Paul Fulton, Ed. D., clinical psychologist.

So, now that we know we have an active role in planning our lives, how is the blueprint actually created? Dr. Michael Newton, counseling psychologist and master hypnotherapist, magnificently describes our life between lives in his book, Destiny of Souls. Here he details the soul's process as it makes plans for the upcoming lifetime and just as Plotinus described, while on The Other Side, when we deem fit, we consult with our spirit guides and begin to develop a detailed design for our next life. Each lifetime's experiences remain in the memory of our collective soul, our Higher Self, which is recorded in the Book of Lives; however, when we inhabit a new human body, we lose temporary access to those memories. If we were to maintain the memories of potentially hundreds of previous lives, we would lose proper perspective while trying to learn the lessons of the current lifetime. Imagine if you were to have the memories of Jeffrey Dahmer in your collection and you were currently living the life of a school teacher. The attitudes and prejudices you once lived with would cloud your decision-making and overall experience in this lifetime.

Few would argue that the Creator is omniscient, having perfect awareness of all of our thoughts and actions and holding the capacity to know everything infinitely. Few would also argue that the Creator is all-loving; therefore, it could be said that the Creator is pure intellect and pure love. However, He is also static, never moving, yet always present. Given that He is static, how would He experience his knowledge? German philosopher Immanuel Kant stated, "It is beyond a doubt that all of our knowledge begins with experience." He believed that using reason without applying it to experience only leads to illusions and he went further to say, "Experience without theory is blind, but theory without experience is mere intellectual play." With this notable difference between intellect and knowledge, how would the Creator turn pure intellect into true knowledge? He experiences knowledge through us, his creations. We are the emotional side of Him. "We are God having a human experience," Teilhard de Chardin. Human beings embody his love and emotion, not separately from Him, but as the actual essence of Him. We are the experiencing, emotional God himself. Our job is to experience life and learn the true meaning of truth and love through our relationships. Everything we do and experience is about learning to love. To do so is the most important task set before us. God created physical worlds as places for us to gain knowledge and perfect our soul. This world is then, in a sense, our schoolhouse, complete with challenges and tests, where we are the students and life is the teacher. Simply living in this negative environment helps us move toward perfection and perfection of the soul is the definitive goal. The way to this perfection is by living in an imperfect world, choosing moral integrity over vice, and using every opportunity afforded us to grow and learn. This is the perfection, the divine order.

"One word frees us of all the weight and pain of life; that word is love."

SOPHOCLES

It is true, God is omniscient, pure intellect, and we were created from Him, nonetheless, we are not to be thought of as perfect in our human form because we are not his perfect intellect. Because we are not pure intellect, we must learn through experience and use that experience to work toward soul evolution. The idea here is that true experience, combined with free will, cannot be accomplished in a perfect environment, such as The Other Side. We must inhabit a place where such growth can take place, a place like planet Earth. The very word "Earth" refers to "chaos" and the term "cosmos" refers to "order". As human beings we have been given free will to make choices that will further our spiritual growth. These choices often knock us off track emotionally when not balanced with intellectual awareness. Free will is the ability to choose our own course. Free will allows us to determine the details of our path. It is our destiny to live out our pre-determined chart and return to the divine; however, free will allows us to determine what the scenery will look like along the way.

It is also true, the Creator is pure love; therefore, because we were created in this likeness, we were created from pure love and all creation begins with a thought. "The ancestor to every action is a thought," wrote Ralph Waldo Emerson, American philosopher. Each soul was created in this same manner and each soul, or thought, was designed to assist with the understanding of pure knowledge, beyond pure intellect. Pure intellect without experience is empty and does not equate to pure knowledge. Aristotle, student of Plato, wrote, "Anything we have to learn to do, we learn by the actual doing of it." For example, if you read a book on how to fly an airplane, does that mean you could immediately operate one safely? Although the intelligence is an important component, it is not enough by itself to complete the task. One learns to walk, by walking. To physically do something is entirely different from simply learning about it. As the Chinese proverb so clearly states, "I hear and I forget, I see and I remember,

I do and I understand." One must experience something fully in order to understand, thus experience becomes the pathway from pure intellect into actual wisdom. Another common day example is the mystery of pre-fabricated, do-it-yourself furniture. Even after diligently reading the instructions and toiling over the complicated diagrams, the ominous task still often grows tedious and we find ourselves resorting to trial and error. The hands-on experience becomes the device through which we learn, grow and ultimately enjoy success.

Creation is made first by a thought and because we were created as these inquiries, or ideas, we were created with an ignorance, a not-knowing. Otherwise, the thought would never have been created. This again is the purpose of our human existence, to experience knowledge beyond pure intellect and to add to the evolution of the collective soul. We are each part of the collective soul, yet we each have our own experiences. These individual experiences are designed to add to the knowledge base of the collective soul. The collective soul holds the knowledge for all of the lifetimes lived by all living beings. Thus, we are all working together to evolve toward perfection. Just as the NDE survivor stated previously, "… the colored drops were the experiences of all who had lived. The experiences existed as separate items yet belonged to the whole. The whole was the collective knowledge of all."

To summarize, the Source is like a river and we are each droplets of water which represent individual thoughts. We are all connected, all flowing together toward a common goal. This might also explain why so many near-death experiences are equated to the feeling of floating down a river. A Buddhist axiom describes our human existence as, "many boats, one river". Ecclesiastes 1:7 reads, "All streams flow into the sea, yet the sea is never full. To the place the streams come from, there they return again." We are all part of the river and essentially part of the Source itself. From whence you came, so shall you return.

"There is a river, the streams whereof
shall make glad the city of God."

Psalms 46:4

Understanding this divine plan makes all the difference between the seemingly random confusion of life and living a well-informed life of purpose. The more we know about the meaning of life, the better we understand the importance of the choices we make in our everyday lives. Just knowing we actually had a choice, that we chose our life challenges, instead of having them arbitrarily inflicted on us, can be of enormous comfort. This understanding is also an invaluable tool in recognizing death, not as an ending, but simply as a transition in the ongoing, eternal intellectual journey of our spirits.

"The last to be overcome is death and the knowledge of life is the knowledge of death."

EDGAR CAYCE

Chapter 2

The Divine Design

"We choose our joys and our sorrows long before we experience them."

Kahlil Gibran

We come to this world as volunteers with a specific task for each lifetime, essentially, a set of goals for the lessons we most need to learn. These goals are detailed in the blueprint that we create with our spirit guides and other spiritual hierarchies in the spirit world. They assist us in selecting the best possible scenarios for learning our deepest desires. The objective is always spiritual evolution and adding to the knowledge of the collective soul. Again, we do maintain the knowledge gained from each lifetime in our psyche, however, while in human form we are only privy to the information gained since that conception. The "forgetfulness" has purpose. Previous experiences would blur the judgment of decisions made during this experience, thus, impeding the learning process. We learn through experience during each lifetime, while tackling the assigned tasks and pursuing the desired knowledge. We then return to the spirit world where we evaluate our progress and, if so desired, begin to create a new plan for further development.

Each lifetime has a different theme, which is called a life theme. There are forty-four life themes listed in world-renowned psychic Sylvia Browne's book, The Other Side and Back. These are life "purposes" which provide the particulars for our experiences. When we devise our blueprint on The Other Side, we choose two of these forty-four themes for our upcoming existence on Earth. One of them is a primary theme, which is who we are, and the other is a secondary theme, which is what we are here to work on, or essentially our life's biggest challenge. Every person carries a major and minor theme through life. These themes play a significant role in the attitudes and tendencies of each person. For example, my major life theme this time is Intellectuality and my secondary theme is Patience. Intellectuality can be described as an ultimate thirst-for-knowledge in which the person studies throughout their life and continuously uses this wealth of information to advance, cultivate, enlighten and expand life on Earth. Patience ranks as one of the more challenging themes because it requires great diligence in a world where impatience is often considered a commendable coping skill. When the Patience theme is selected, it indicates fervor to move more quickly along the spiritual journey than someone who has chosen a less hurried theme. Therefore, Patience also indicates somewhat of a spiritual impatience.

For purposes of duality, each theme also has a flipside that can override any benefit gained. The Intellectuality theme could lead a person to become a "professional student" with the sole goal of acquisition of knowledge and without the desire to share that knowledge, which renders it useless to anyone except that individual. Also, this theme heavily challenges the person to maintain a balance of both work and play in their life. The Patience theme could lead to a constant battle with guilt, guilt resulting from any feelings of anger or frustration that were expressed or suppressed during moments of impatience. This is where our free will is called to action. If you were to evaluate the recurring challenges in your everyday life, you would certainly find a common thread. That thread is directly tied to your life themes and the lessons you set out to learn this lifetime.

The other forty-two life themes include: Activator, Aesthetic Pursuits, Analyzer, Banner Carrier, Builder, Catalyst, Cause Fighter, Controller, Emotionality, Experiencer, Fallibility, Follower, Harmony, Healer, Humanitarian, Infallibility, Irritant, Justice, Lawfulness, Leader, Loner, Loser, Manipulator, Passivity, Pawn, Peacemaker, Performance, Persecution, Persecutor, Poverty, Psychic, Rejection, Rescuer, Responsibility, Spirituality, Survival, Temperance, Tolerance, Victim, Victimizer, Warrior and Winner. And, not to lessen any of them because they are all equally important, some of the most intriguing themes to me include Emotionality, Irritant, Loser, Poverty, Warrior and Winner because when I first read the descriptions years ago, I was able to immediately put faces to the words and this has helped me reach a deeper understanding of the people involved. People born with an Emotionality theme have an extraordinary ability to feel every shade of emotion, from the highest high to the lowest low. This sensitivity is both a gift and a burden to them and they must strive to maintain balance between the two extremes. It was also comforting to me to know that there was a category for Irritants. We all know people that fit into this category. They are the incessant complainers, the people that seem to find fault in everything. They serve as excellent teachers for us with constant lessons of tolerance and patience, all the while struggling to overcome this very negativity in their own life. Losers, outside of the derogatory title, are those that feel sorry for themselves and often become martyrs. They thrive on drama and will do anything to keep that drama in their life. Similar to Irritants, they encourage us to keep a positive outlook on life and to live without judgment.

Knowledge of the Poverty theme also brought comfort and enlightenment to my mind. Apparent poverty takes place in third world countries and in certain regions of our own country, but it also takes place in the midst of affluence. Here, even the privileged struggle to satisfy their needs because they never feel as if they have enough. A focus on their own spiritual path, rather than on accumulation, will spur personal growth. Warriors are our unsung heroes and, in a time of war, it is nice to know that this was a deep-seeded need for this group. They include our soldiers and any other risk-takers willing to step up to the physical and spiritual challenge of combating crime, abuses and natural disasters. If Warriors are able to properly channel their aggression, they are often able to make significant contributions to our history. Winners are those eternal optimists always encouraged by the next best thing. They are able to inspire positivity, yet they are often threatened with the risk of losing everything.

I strongly encourage you to review the totality of the life themes and discover the ones that match your patterns. Grasping the rationale behind the eternal choices you made will help you better understand your greatest challenges and possibly lead you to be more forgiving of yourself. We must also keep in mind that one of the chief reasons we plan life challenges is to be of service to others, with the overall ambition being to increase the collective consciousness; yet, as we say, charity begins at home. If you are able to better understand your own challenges, you will be further equipped to make decisions that support your own chosen theme and the themes selected by those around you without trepidation or judgment.

Not only did we select a primary and secondary life theme, we also selected our genetic code, our birthplace and our birthparents. All of the different cultures of the world exist to teach tolerance and we chose the race and the culture in which we would begin life for very specific reasons. All of these pre-birth decisions set up the environment in which we would be most apt to learn our desired life lessons. For example, if you chose to be born into a family in a war-torn country, possibly your goal was to learn a lesson of true justice, equality or tolerance. Perhaps you chose to be born into an affluent family with a trust fund, where work was not a requirement. Your challenge then might be to overcome a sense of entitlement or to develop a sense of self, outside of the family name. Possibly you chose to be born into a mid-western family where a particular rigid religious belief was dominant. This might present an opportunity to develop a sense of belonging or a chance to strike out on your own spiritual journey. Maybe you chose to be born into a tribal community somewhere in sub-Saharan Africa. Your lesson here might pertain to nurturing an appreciation for your surroundings, a love for the land or for a simpler lifestyle. This choice may also relate to developing empathy for others and cultivating a deeper level of compassion. Possibly you chose to be the third child behind two very successful siblings. This choice would provide challenges of personal awareness and acceptance. Perhaps you chose to be the only child born to two emotionally unavailable parents. Lessons here may pertain to working through resentment or feelings of self-importance. For me, as the youngest of six children and witness to five older siblings struggling through their formative years, all the while utilizing every possible coping device, issues of perfectionism were brought to the forefront, where I learned very quickly which path I was not willing to travel and what I felt was necessary to maintain both my individuality and my independence.

"Mother Nature provides the proper climate for the seed to grow. She does not tell the seed what to become."

UNKNOWN

Every single piece of the puzzle selected during the pre-birth planning was purposeful. Specifics including astrological sign, birth year, birth order, number of siblings and parental traits all play a major role in the development of the personality and the conditioning received during our formative years. Any minor adjustment to that plan would have had an extraordinarily dramatic effect on the outcome. Here again lies the perfection in the plan. Even the most minute details were scripted into your play. How you live out that script is all about the interpretation of the experience. Our perceptions often create somewhat of an optical delusion for us, which creates a sort of personal prison. Epictetus, Greek philosopher, wrote, "Men are disturbed not by the things that happen, but by their opinion of the things that happen." The manner in which you interpret your experience is a choice and the choice is yours. The choice is always yours.

As you can see, while we are on this agreed upon journey there are never any right or wrong choices. There are simply choices.

There are no mistakes, only experiences. Henry Ford, American businessman, said, "Failure is the opportunity to begin again more intelligently." Failure is only a bad thing when you equate it to your self-worth. In actuality, failure is merely one step toward the right answer. Failure simply refers to the state or condition of not meeting an intended objective; therefore, once we realize we did not reach our target, we can begin again with new focus. Everything and everyone around us constantly provides us with an opportunity to learn, we simply need to recognize it as such and use the knowledge to further our growth. This is part of the perfection. Everything is exactly as it should be in this very moment. Everything that you encounter was placed there for you. Only you. Only you are living this exact experience with this exact knowledge base and that, in itself, is quite amazing.

"We are a landscape of all we have seen."

Isamu Noguchi

Each of us carries inside a little bit of everyone and everything we have ever come in contact with throughout our life. Every encounter provides information, knowledge. The option to gain value from each encounter is only missed if we do not take notice. We also waste the opportunity when we add judgment or anger that clouds our view. Oftentimes, we think of events in our lives as happening *to* us, not *for* us. Life is not happening *to* us, life is *responding* to us. Life is a process, not an event. We are simply here to experience. The interpretation of that experience is key to our evolution. This very reason is why living a fully conscious life is so vital.

Let's discuss a common encounter in most of our lives. Let's say that you are in line at a grocery store. The line is quite long and you, naturally, are in somewhat of a hurry. Has anyone ever gone to the grocery store when they weren't in a hurry? Anyway, you look around for other open lanes, only to discover that you are already in line for the only open check stand. Despite the one employee feverishly trying to keep up with the demand, you notice two employees huddled near the door. They appear to be engaged in a deep conversation, one that does not pertain to business. Your mind begins to race and you attempt to make eye contact with the other people in line. You are hoping to share your disgust with them and feel that validation that comes from a collective disapproval. You begin to make those stifled grunt noises, all meant to subtly show your dissatisfaction. You advance to mumbling under your breath. You utter things like, "Why me?", "Why does this always happen to me?" and "Why does this always happen when I'm in a hurry?" Does this scenario sound vaguely familiar?

In order to learn from this encounter, we must understand the dynamics of the experience. First and foremost, we must always look for our own responsibility in the moment. What role did you play in this scene? Running late and possibly choosing to shop during the store's busiest hours were choices you made long before your arrival at the store. Those choices had absolutely nothing to do with anyone in that store, even the two huddled employees. These choices helped create the urgency you felt, the victimization you felt and the disrespect you felt. All of those occurrences were in your own hands. The law of attraction also comes into play here. Like attracts like, therefore, your hurried state of mind sought out a similar, comfortable, compatible scenario. Although, in this example it is clear to see how our own actions create the moments of our lives, as humans we are more likely to place blame outside of ourselves and project our frustrations onto others. The fault here would likely have been placed on the non-attentive employees for not jumping to our rescue, or on the store manager for not staffing the store appropriately, or on all of the people driving the cars that got in our way in route to the store.

Each moment has purpose. These seemingly average moments make up our lives. They make up the experience. These moments do not happen to us, they happen for us. Among the lessons of the grocery store scene were patience and tolerance. In those everyday moments, we learn. In those everyday moments, we grow. In those everyday moments, we add to the collective knowledge. We often make choices without ever even contemplating the impact they may have on others, but we also make choices without realizing the impact they have on ourselves. Lessons are meant to be learned. If not, they are repeated, just like grade school levels. They are repeated until they are mastered, therefore, it would benefit each one of us and all of humanity to master our lessons. When we learn a lesson it adds to the evolution of consciousness, which in turn also helps us individually. When another grows in love, so do I. It is as if we are thrown to Earth at the lowest vibrational level and we have to work our way up the ladder to the highest rung, which is love. "Do not despise the bottom rungs in the ascent to greatness," advised Latin writer, Publilius Syrus. Love is the absolute highest vibration and God is perfect love.

"Love is the greatest power on Earth. It conquers all things."

Peace Pilgrim

Once we begin to live in an aware or awakened state, we learn how to interpret our experiences and discover our lessons. The apprehension and judgment fade away and are readily replaced with acknowledgment and appreciation. When this occurs, there is a brilliant shift that takes place from blame to responsibility to understanding. This understanding leads to gratitude and gratitude removes blame from our lives. It is easy to be thankful during the good times, but it demonstrates great wisdom to be able to display gratitude even during our most challenging moments.

A fully conscious person, if implanted into the same grocery store scene, would make a concerted effort to survey the scene for the lesson, without ever jumping on the blame wagon. They may have come to the conclusion that the "slow down" was a universal suggestion to take notice of their life as it occurred, rather than hurrying through it without thought. They may have distinguished it as one of those "in the moment" training opportunities, which continually remind us to live in the here and now. Whatever the case, they would be able to realize the impact of the choices they made leading up to that very hectic moment in line and they would be able to find meaning in that moment. They would also find solace in discovering the lesson, as opposed to missing it, and in taking another step toward perfection in the evolution of their soul. All of our reactions are based on the interpretation of the experience. Interpretations are choices. In this case, one interpretation was the role of offended victim and another interpretation was the role of appreciative student. Yet again, the choice is always yours.

How would your interpretation of the above situation have changed if, at the time, you were aware that the busy clerk was nervously brand new, that three other employees had failed to show up for their scheduled shift, or that the two huddled employees had been off the clock for over forty-five minutes and that they were both waiting near the door, largely to avoid the driving rain that had just begun to fall, as they waited for the bus to take them home to their respective homes and frightened children that were alone and hungry? Would you have a different perspective on your own importance? Or, on the urgency of your task at hand? Or, on the overall state of affairs? In this physical plane, you will rarely know the specific details of all that is happening around you or that which is happening in the lives of those around you. Everyone is fighting a battle and this simple fact begs for acts of kindness and compassion. The choice is always yours on how to read the scene and how to react. You may choose to empathize with the worker and work on your own patience and lessons or you may spend your time feeling like a victim, never realizing the episode had intended purpose specifically for you. One choice moves you forward and brings you peace while the other almost guarantees that you will experience similar situations again and again until you see the value and take notice of both the lesson and your life.

"We do not see things as they are. We see them as we are."

Anais Nin

Chapter 3

Interpretation is Everything

"There are no facts, only interpretations."

FRIEDRICH NIETZSCHE

Spirituality is about the continual asking of the eternal questions, the unwavering search for purpose in life. The purpose of life is about the actual experiences we go through while living. Therefore, there is a direct connection between spirituality and the interpretation of this experience we call life. We perceive reality in accordance with our level of consciousness and thus our spirituality may be defined by how we interpret our experience. Some interpretations limit our view and hinder our progress. Other interpretations shed light and propel us forward. If the everyday tasks of your life make sense to you and you are able to find meaning even in the mundane, then you have an increased probability of understanding even the most challenging situations that life brings your way. These moments are when our lessons are greatest. If your sense of meaning and purpose is intact, you are more likely to travel through the world virtually emotionally unscathed. The challenging periods in life that all of us go through are the times when we most often question our purpose. Spirituality helps us find deeper meaning in our lives and this knowledge becomes the food of our souls. We search within our soul for the answers because we are aware of its connection to the divine.

"You cannot teach a man anything; you can only help him to find it within himself."

GALILEO

In Buddhism, the physical world is considered to be the object of the mind and Siddhartha Gautama, better known as *the* Buddha, or "the enlightened one", taught Four Noble Truths about all life experience. These four truths are the foundation of Buddhism and they lead to great happiness and spiritual joy once they are fully realized. They are simple and fundamental, yet they are often complicated for the cluttered human mind. The First Noble Truth is the truth of suffering. This can be translated directly into "life is suffering". Most humans want to tune out at this point. No one wants to believe that all life has to offer is pain and agony, but one must realize that through the moments of suffering we learn our greatest lessons. What have you learned during the times of ease in your life? During what periods of your life have you shown the most growth? The resounding answer to that question would be that during your most challenging stages you have also experienced the most spiritual growth. This world is perfect, but only if we understand the perfection. The healthy person finds no reason to consult a doctor and the well-adjusted person rarely finds it important to question the meaning of life. It is only when we suffer misfortune that we begin to question why something has happened. It is true, during our lifetime we will experience various levels of suffering, including both physical pain and psychological pain, but there are also positive experiences that life provides that we generally identify as the opposite of suffering, such as ease, comfort and joy. These moments must also be acknowledged for us to understand the duality of life, that in order for there to be happiness, there must also be sadness, for there to be joy, there must also be pain. Without darkness, one cannot comprehend the light.

The first truth implies impermanence. Nothing lasts. Items emerge on a mythical horizon called the future, they pass by us as mere experiences and, just as swiftly as they appeared, they disappear into a void called the past. The World Series from last year is in the same void as the sinking of the Titanic many years ago. Because there is no permanence, there is no place for anything to rest. Life then is nothing more than a continuous series of adaptations in search of comfort and familiarity. This first truth is deeply rooted in the concept discussed earlier that life is nothing more than the experience itself. The aspect of suffering arrives when we find ourselves searching for that comfort and familiarity. Rather than simply accepting the experiences for what they are, and finding consolation and meaning in that, we continue to search for comfort from our material world, which leads to both pain and suffering. We become attached to the world. We keep emotions and memories tied up in our attachments, thus causing ourselves grave anguish. The concept of impermanence often gets muddled in the unconscious mind because ego keeps it chained to the physical world. The ego is the idea we carry around that makes us believe we are separate from our source, the divine. It believes, "I am what I do" or "I am what I possess". Our ego wraps us in earthly conquests and material possessions and resists our attempts to see the world as fleeting. We take no material possessions with us from lifetime to lifetime, nor do we take them into the spirit world; yet, there is no true lacking at any point in our lives. Lack is an illusion. "When you realize there is nothing lacking, the whole world belongs to you," Lao Tzu, founder of Taoism. The universe in which we live is powerfully and delightfully accommodating. The law of abundance and the law of attraction will provide all that we need, if only we were to ask for it, be willing to work for it and then be patient enough to wait its arrival. We are meant to live lives full of abundance and grace. The trick is knowing what we want, as well as only asking for things that will advance our growth.

Like a physician prescribing a treatment for an ailment, Buddha's first truth identifies the illness and then the second truth explains what may trigger the disease. This Second Noble Truth is the truth of the cause of suffering, which states that the cause of human suffering is the actual act of craving or clinging. The origin of the suffering is in the attachment. We continually search for something outside of ourselves to make us happy, but no matter how much perceived success we enjoy, the craving never subsides. We spend our moments grabbing one article after another in hopes of it providing us with a sense of security, that same sense of comfort and familiarity. We not only find ourselves seeking out tangible products, but also affirming ideas and opinions about ourselves and the world around us. Judgments on our human body have no relevance for our soul. "What strikes the oyster shell does not damage the pearl," wrote Rumi, Persian poet and theologian. The soul is separate and everlasting and the body is only a temporary package utilized to move us through this world. Thomas Edison cleverly said, "The body's only function is to carry the brain around." Nothing that happens on Earth may hurt our soul. A pearl dropped in the mud does not lose its value. Our souls will continue to exist even beyond the use of continuous human forms. Ignorance is the state in which one lacks an understanding of how their mind is attached to these impermanent objects. Once we fully understand that nothing is permanent and that these objects are fleeting, we turn our focus away from the craving and inward to the only permanent existence, our soul.

The Third Noble Truth is the truth of the end of suffering. On a positive note, this truth is holding out hope for the cure. The eradication of suffering *is* attainable, but only through the removal of the cause of suffering. Sounds easy, but this is where most humans only begin to experience what we consider suffering. Through our attachments, lessons are learned, lessons of acceptance and lessons of release, or letting go. Lessons of acceptance deal with our persistent search for validation from others and our surroundings. Lessons of release deal with our ability to remain detached from tangible items and outside opinions. The removal of these cravings, these desires, these wants, is a process that requires great awareness, great strength and continual practice. Simone Weil, French philosopher and mystic, affirmed, "Attachment is the great fabricator of illusions; reality can be attained only by someone who is detached." Detachment is often thought of as something negative in our western world; however, detachment does not equate to 'not loving' something or someone. It actually means quite the opposite. Only when we truly love something or someone are we able to let go completely without causing ourselves pain. Once this detachment is attained, nirvana is reached. Nirvana is defined as a psychological state of freedom from all worries, troubles, personal complexes, fabrications and ideas.

"Anything you strive to hold captive will hold you captive and, if you desire freedom, you must give freedom."

PEACE PILGRIM

The Fourth Noble Truth is the truth of the path that frees us from suffering. Buddha did not hold a pessimistic view of the world, as many want to believe. Yes, he did believe that suffering was inevitable, but he also believed there was hope, that this suffering could be healed through awareness and a new way of thinking. He taught us, "The unenlightened life is suffering," that anyone that does not reach a higher level of consciousness will continue to create their own suffering on Earth. He also said, "The enlightened life is bliss. It is nirvana, free of suffering," and he suggested that, "The door to nirvana is always open," therefore, since nirvana is a state of being free from suffering, we should all work toward enlightenment and a life free of this self-imposed torment.

This path to liberation is the Eight-Fold Path that includes wisdom (right-view and right-thought), ethical conduct (right-speech, right-action and right-livelihood), and mental discipline (right-effort, right-mindfulness and right-concentration). This is a steady path of self-improvement. It may be found at the mid-way point between two extremes, hedonism and asceticism. Hedonism can be described as the self-indulgent pursuit of pleasure as a way of life. Asceticism can be described as living a life of strict self-denial. "When we can accept all of life's contradictions, when we can comfortably flow between the banks of pleasure and pain, experiencing them both while getting stuck in neither, then we are free," Deepak Chopra, American physician and philosopher. This mid-point is where we find balance, a center. This is where all of the cravings, ignorance, delusions and their effects will disappear gradually as progress is made along the spiritual path. This process is gradual and often takes place over the period of several lifetimes.

The Four Noble Truths appear to be quite simple in writing, though we, as ego-driven human beings, need immense practice to even begin to live the concepts outlined. As previously stated, intellectual awareness is simply not enough. Experience is necessary in order to turn intellect into true knowledge and this transformation comes from the combination of the actual experience and the acknowledgement and deciphering of that experience. In Buddhist texts, this transformation is the development of wisdom, the first step along the Eight-Fold Path. You must seek not only knowledge, but also wisdom. Wisdom is the ability to fully understand and utilize the acquired knowledge. Although we are not able to physically see wisdom, we can certainly see its likeness in acts of kindness, compassion, fearlessness and peacefulness.

"Life is not an amateur circus tent where those who enter are individual, lonely performers with no script and no director, only a tumbling about, a fling through the air, and then a crash. No, that is false. As souls, you are self-determining. You decide when to be born. You create your life every minute of every day by what you choose to believe. You decide when to die. All things evolve around the total truth of love, balance, order, cause and effect. These are Divine laws."

Pat Rodegast

How we choose to respond to the world around us determines the quality of our lives. We each have the power to create our own heaven on Earth or our own hell on Earth. We choose to live in a hostile world or a friendly world and then we spend our lives looking for ways to validate that belief. When we designed our blueprint, we included challenges that will inevitably generate both peaks and valleys. The design process can be likened to planning a road trip from San Diego, California to Orlando, Florida. The destination has been set, but the route is undetermined. You can choose to leave San Diego and head directly north toward Canada, you can head directly south toward Mexico, or you can point yourself in the exact direction of Florida and hit the gas. You can whine about the car you are driving, the food you are provided, the rain you encounter, the people you meet, the music on the radio or the hotel beds. Or, you can thoroughly appreciate the reliability of the vehicle, the chance to try new types of cuisine, the nourishment the rain provides nature, the uniqueness and joy in the faces of the people you meet, the opportunity to discover a new artist on the radio and the way you love to watch television from bed. How we choose to view the experience is a choice of vision. We will all face challenges, that is inescapable, but the focus should move toward extracting as much value as we possibly can from each and every moment.

Once set, the final destination of this earthly trip may not be altered. The destination was determined before conception and cannot be changed once you are in human form. Fortunately, no matter which route you decide to take, you cannot fail. In other words, you will get yourself from San Diego to Orlando. It may not be pretty or it may be unimaginably smooth, nonetheless, you will get there. We will always fulfill our charts, but often out of poor judgment we delay our own progress by choosing to take the rough road when a perfectly smooth road is nearby. For instance, in the road trip example, you may have opted for a bicycle instead of an automobile, or you may have selected to walk the grueling distance, rather than utilizing some form of motorized transportation. You might have chosen to wear shoes that were too big, or selected a bicycle with a wobbly frame or a slow-leaking tire. You might have chosen to leave the much-needed umbrella behind or to travel without a change of clothing. These are choices of free will, choices that reflect the specific details of the trip. Nevertheless, in the long run, you will meet your desired challenges. You will arrive at your pre-set destination and, knowing your inevitable success, the fear of failure diminishes. This knowing makes life joyous and purposeful.

Now that the spotlight is no longer on *whether* you have a pre-birth plan, but *why* you have the plan, you can turn your attention toward improving the quality of your journey. The focus should now be on the daily decisions you make and how they guide your life. The single most significant power we own is the power of decision. Mastering oneself is true power and how you live in this world is ultimately the measure of your spiritual maturity. Spirituality has little to do with what you know or how many books you have read. It has everything to do with how you move through the world, your daily behavior and how aware you are in every single moment. Mahatma Gandhi, former political and spiritual leader of India, told us that, "Happiness is when what you think, what you say, and what you do are in harmony." This world is where your spiritual work is done and the day-to-day implementation of your values will ease the impact from any bumps you might encounter along the way. However, living according to our own set of ethics can be challenging in this world of shallowness and despair. Civil law dictates our actions somewhat, so, even though we have free will, we are not completely free to act as we wish. We have a duty to each other to behave in ways that benefit all of mankind. Our free will allows us to choose our character and what type of person we will become. It also allows us to determine how we will treat others, how much we will learn, what we will accomplish, our attitude toward our environment, our belief system and our personal set of values. When we act according to our own principles, we feel at peace. When we are at peace, there are no longer internal struggles that skew our perspective and knock us off balance.

"To put the world right in order, we must first put the nation in order; to put the nation in order, we must first put the family in order; to put the family in order, we must first cultivate our personal life; we must first set our hearts right."

Confucius

If you are currently unsure what your personal code of conduct entails, I encourage you to take a moment to list the values you place in high regard, the values you respect in others and the behavior you expect from yourself. This is your personal value system and it should be reflected in your daily actions. The Buddhist concept of "right-action" is when you choose to do what is right even when no one is watching and no one may ever find out. In those moments, you still choose to do what you believe in your heart is right. Those around you deduce what your beliefs are by evaluating your actions. They will not have to guess what you are against, if they clearly know what you support. Inquire with your family and friends what they feel you believe. Their responses will reveal your behavior, but be careful not to interrupt during their responses, simply listen. Absorb what they are saying and learn from the experience. If what they say is out of synch with what you believe, your actions must be reviewed. When what we do is out of synch with what we believe, we are not on track with our chart. We often act mindlessly without ever realizing the impact of our actions. Living what you believe puts you back in step with your purpose and that, in itself, will bring you great joy.

We must, as always, look upon ourselves first because, as a people, we tend to create a significant amount of undue stress by the manner in which we interpret situations. Interpretation is everything. Each individual on Earth is essentially living in their own world, their own world within a world. How we perceive our current surroundings is directly correlated to all of our past experiences, combined with all of the knowledge that we have previously acquired and infused with our personal attitudes and prejudices. For example, if eight people were to witness an automobile accident, each witness would have observed a different accident, the same accident albeit, but from a different point of view. They would each have their own individualized interpretation of what occurred. The varying angles and degrees of sight would play a significant role, as would the level of attention paid by each witness. No two interpretations would be the same. Doesn't this deepen your appreciation for law enforcement officers left with the task of sorting out and searching for the truth based on the varied experiences? Their mission is reflective of the task we each face in our lives, the search for that elusive truth based on our interpretations and experiences.

Another example of how perception varies greatly from person to person and what role it plays in our decision-making process comes from a recent news report. The story involved a local elementary school teacher and a gun that was discovered in her classroom. Her perception was that she was protecting the children by having the weapon at the ready. She thought that if danger came from the outside, she would use the firearm to protect the children and switch the focus onto herself, allowing the students to escape unharmed. Sadly, this particular teacher had already been involved in a separate school shooting scenario in which she was unable to protect her students. Her past experience had filled her with fear, which clouded her vision. Her intention was appropriate; however, her actions were bewildering. Societal law will place judgment on her actions only, not on her intentions, while our own personal values hinge on our intentions. Fear clouded her awareness and her actions were out of line with what her intentions were, therefore, she was working against her chart.

Perception is different for everyone. Some people find riding a roller coaster to be extremely stressful, while others find it exhilarating. Some will climb to the top of a majestic mountain and only speak of the frigid air. Others will climb that same mountain and gaze for hours at the astonishing view. You have been gifted with the free will to choose how you will react in every situation. It all depends on your perspective. I have a friend who is a chronic worrier and although, to her credit, she is working diligently on taking notice of her first reaction and not acting upon it without a purposeful pause, her mindset generally sprints to the negative in nearly every situation. My mindset, on the other hand, is the complete opposite. My mind races to the positive and immediately begins to problem-solve. I am the eternal optimist drinking from the half-full glass with complete confidence there is plenty more in the refrigerator. I stopped allowing my emotions to run my life long ago. I prefer to remain patient and hopeful about what the change will bring my way. There is a great deal of power in the pause. Taking a purposeful pause allows me to interpret the situation rationally, rather than emotionally. We must be slow to anger. Reacting, without evaluating the scene or the true intention, can be foolish and regretful and often leads to missing out on the actual lesson provided. This is just one way we create unnecessary stress for ourselves through misguided or uninformed interpretations, which may also be called assumptions. Recognizing how frequently we act mindlessly as humans, a purposeful pause allows us the chance to remove judgment from our reaction, and, in the meantime, waiting until the end of the story before reacting keeps us from contemplating all of the possible distressing endings that may or may not come to fruition.

"If you think the worst and get the worst, you suffer twice.
If you think the best and get the worst, you suffer once."

Anonymous

The following renowned Taoist story exemplifies the significance of keeping a proper perspective, of evaluating the entire story and not writing the ending before it has occurred, and for taking that purposeful pause before reacting. The story involves a farmer and his horse. A horse was stolen from a poor farmer. His neighbors quickly expressed their sympathy at his assumed misfortune. The farmer replied, "How do you know this isn't a good thing?" A few months passed and the horse returned to the farmer, bringing along a mate. Soon the farmer had many horses and became very wealthy. The neighbors applauded his good fortune. The farmer replied, "How do you know this isn't a bad thing?" One day, the farmer's son went riding on their finest horse. The son fell off the horse, broke his hip and was permanently crippled. The neighbors arrived to offer their condolences. The farmer replied, "How do you know this isn't a good thing?" Soon, war came to the region and all of the able-bodied young men were sent off to battle. Nine out of the ten men died in action. The farmer's son, because he was crippled, had avoided combat and lived to a ripe old age in great prosperity.

This fable teaches us that the story never really ends, for as long as life persists, something new will happen next. No matter what has happened to you or around you, there is always more to the story that your ego might not see or understand. The farmer was able to take each experience for what it was in the moment. He was able to maintain perspective, never projecting his worries into the story. He simply let the story unfold and watched the magic take place. Everything truly does happen for a reason, even if we are unable to detect that reason initially. There is always more story on the way.

"There is nothing good or bad but thinking makes it so."

SHAKESPEARE

As we go about allowing our lives to unfold, inevitably small struggles will occur that bring about varying degrees of reactions. One must be careful not to overreact without having all of the necessary pieces of the puzzle or without understanding the true intentions of the other involved parties. Overreacting generally stems from judgment and invariably leads to feelings of guilt and regret, feelings that could have been avoided through a conscious effort to simply pause before allowing our emotions to take control. The next time you feel uptight or anxious consider the origin of that emotion. First, only think in terms of you, not about the other person or any additional parties. Contemplate what the emotion is revealing about you. Do not judge yourself, simply identify the feeling. Remember, each encounter provides you with an opportunity to grow, to learn a lesson. This reflection will lead to awareness and the next time you are faced with this same type of situation, you will be better equipped to handle it more constructively. "Everything that happens to you is your teacher. The secret is to learn to sit at the feet of your own life and be taught by it. Everything that happens is either a blessing, which is also a lesson, or a lesson which is also a blessing," Polly Berends, American author. The choice is always yours to either acknowledge and learn the lesson, or to simply ignore it, only to see the lesson repeated again and again until you do take notice.

Oftentimes, our intentions are good but our actions are erroneous. There is an immense difference between a harmful act that was done maliciously and one that was done inadvertently. The divine source knows our hearts and our souls and is most concerned with our intentions. "The Lord does not look at the things man looks at. Man looks at outward appearance but the Lord looks at the heart," I Samuel 16:7. We must act accordingly. We will always find ourselves in the position of being able to add to or subtract from the value of every situation we encounter. We constantly face choices that make us either part of the problem or part of the solution. A simple, compassionate philosophy to live by is to "above all else, be kind". We must apply love whenever possible. If you see hatred, respond with love. If you see anger, respond with love. If you see intolerance, respond with love. If you do not respond with love, and instead you choose to respond in the same manner, a vicious cycle of pain will continue without relief. This type of response would also place you on the same level as the other person, a place that holds the very thing you were judging. Instead, choose to be part of the solution. Stop the cycle. Demonstrate love. Mother Teresa once said, "Let no one ever come to you without leaving better and happier." Whenever you leave a scene or a friend, you should attempt to leave them better than they were before you arrived. This will create a trail of kindness and peace for everyone you encounter and it will place you on the path toward illumination.

"Each person must live their life as a model for others."

Rosa Parks

The actual interpretation of the scene is what determines our actions, or our next move. Take a purposeful pause each time you begin to experience an emotional reaction. This pause will allow you a chance to get past or through the emotions to your rational side. Consider your own role in the outcome. Consider your own actions. Consider your own intentions. Were they in line with each other? Were your actions motivated by love, peace and kindness or were they motivated by greed, fear and judgment? When you feel the urge to react, take a brief pause to contemplate whether this will matter in ten minutes, ten hours or even ten months. Most of the time, you will discover it will not matter at all. Learning to take that pause can be difficult because it relies on your awareness level. You must first catch yourself reacting and then choose to think positively. You must also consider why you are reacting this particular way. What is motivating your choice? How little does it actually have to do with the other people involved? This simple pause, this act of awareness, often takes you out of the victim role and puts you in the driver's seat. This is where we gain proper perspective. This is where we learn to make constructive decisions. This is where we either create or alleviate that undue suffering. We create tension for ourselves because we are unwilling to think, to take the time to reflect upon the situation or to see the situation for what it is and move on with appreciation. As a nation, we are not great thinkers. We certainly have a lot of intelligent people, but we are not great thinkers. We rush through life. We have numerous routines that keep us from thinking and we have countless machines that think for us. Studies show that nearly 90% of our lives is spent in routine. Being mindful is the goal. Being in the moment leads to awareness and awareness leads to enlightenment.

Once you begin to notice your life in this capacity, your perspective, as well as your priorities, will change. What you used to find yourself focused on will shift. You will experience a glorious transfer from one of aspiration, or ambition, to a more meaningful, purpose-driven focus. You will move out of the sphere of achievement into the sphere of enjoyment. This is similar to the shift we all experience throughout the decades of our lives. We are typically ego-driven through our 20s and that begins to transform into self-discovery during our 30s, which eventually leads to an increased drive to live a life of service in our 40s and beyond. In a sense, we experience a complete transformation during each lifetime.

"The man who views the world at fifty, the same as he did at twenty, has wasted thirty years of his life."

MUHAMMAD ALI

During this transformation, your priorities will change and your actions will inevitably reflect that change. The reaction that the impatient person next to you in rush hour traffic would have received will be replaced by one of service, one that understands that the majority of people are really only after happiness, which in this case is the ability to switch lanes, get to their loved ones, avoid being late to their job, etc. Once this person's wish is granted, they generally move on without further concern. The fact that that person may have left late in the first place, or that they appear to consider themselves more important than those around them, well, that is their karma, not yours. Their actions are not a personal attack against you. Most of the time, if questioned, they would not even be able to identify your face. They were so focused on their own needs that they did not even notice those around them. Do you really think they were thinking about you and that they were seriously making an attempt to ruin your day? Absolutely not. Honestly, they probably never even gave you a second thought, while you sat and marinated in your own bitterness. We should never take another person's actions personally, which is part of the contract for personal freedom as spelled out in The Four Agreements by Don Miguel Ruiz. This guide includes the following personal agreements: be impeccable with your word, never take anything personally, never make assumptions and always do your best. "Others are going to have their own belief system, so nothing they think about me is really about me, but it is about them," writes Ruiz. We often find ourselves taking things personally because we buy into what is being said. We all live in our own little world, different from each other, and when we take something personally we are assuming that the other person knows what is in our world. Thus, we project, or impose, our world onto their world. If we are able to separate ourselves from the actions of others, we will deny ourselves a significant amount of unnecessary grief; however, we often get caught up in working for the morality police, when we might otherwise choose to add to the situation and simply leave it alone. Instead, we whip out that badge, escalating the situation into something it never needed to be. But, keep in mind, if you do choose to help the situation, you are helping not only yourself, but the others around you and that is service and that will bring you peace.

This shift in priorities is a beautiful transformation. The nature of life on Earth is constant change and the more you are able to work with the changes, rather than fighting them, you will be able to use life as a teacher and flow with whatever comes your way. There will always be more mountains to climb, but you will be able to see the lesson in each obstacle. However, if there were no mountains to climb, there would be no lessons to learn and essentially no spiritual growth.

"After illumination, difficulties continue to arise; what changes is your relationship to them. You see more and resist less. You gain the capacity to turn your problems into lessons and your lessons into wisdom."

SOCRATES

Chapter 4

Karmic Lessons

"If there is a God, why is there so much good?
If there is a God, why is there so much evil?"

St. Augustine

It is nearly impossible to think about the purpose of life without also thinking about the purpose for all of the suffering. Even the Bible includes stories of people who questioned the purpose of their life, i.e., Job. In his book, Man's Search for Meaning, Viktor E. Frankl, Holocaust survivor, stated, "If there is a meaning in life at all, then there must be a meaning in suffering. Suffering is an ineradicable part of life, even as fate and death." He also wrote, "There is nothing in this world, I venture to say, that would so effectively help one survive even the worst conditions as the knowledge there is meaning in one's life." Suffering teaches compassion. Without suffering and the search for compassion, there would be no need for life lessons, thus no need for the human experience. The physical world, as we know it, was created, not as a place of endless suffering, but as a schoolhouse for us to experience life and love and for us to use this knowledge to assist in the evolution of the collective soul. When we return to the spirit world, each and every one of us benefits from our experience on Earth. While in physical form, we have all, at one time or another, empathetically watched the evening news or picked up a newspaper and uttered the question, "Why did this happen?" We have all witnessed a devastating incident and wondered the reason. We have all questioned why seemingly bad things happen to good people. But, in order to make sense of these events, we must first further explore the concept of dualism.

Duality can be defined as the state of having two equivalent natures, i.e., hot and cold, up and down, good and bad, as in yin yang, the Chinese symbol for two opposing but equal forces. Yin equals darkness (moon/womanhood) and yang equals light (sun/manhood). They are complementary opposites within a greater whole. This dichotomy illustrates the fact that in order to experience happiness, we must also experience sorrow, for without one, the other has no effect. In order to experience the joys, we must also be willing to touch the sadness. If we have never touched true sorrow, how would we be able to know true joy? If we have never encountered hatred, how would we be able to expand our understanding of compassion and love? If we have never experienced deep pain, how would we be able to recognize authentic pleasure? Even love can bring us the most severe pain, yet the most beautiful joy. That balance is necessary. Without one, we do not have the other. We must be able to compare and contrast before we are able to fully realize the value. There is a Buddhist saying, "Life is full of 10,000 joys and 10,000 sorrows." This proverb describes a balancing of experiences, in other words, duality.

In our western culture, karma is a word that has lost its true meaning. Over the years, many belief systems have professed the idea of sin as a wrongdoing that will eventually lead to severe consequences. This thought has led many to unnecessarily endure excessive amounts of fear and guilt. The word sin simply means to "miss the mark". Therefore, if you miss the experience of learning, karma will make sure the lesson comes around again. This universal law allows you to have continual chances to repeat the lesson until you are able to cleanly hit the mark. Edgar Cayce confirmed, "An error we refuse to correct has many lives." You may find yourself wanting to change locations to avoid this karma, but the lesson will follow you wherever you go until it is fully realized. We are here on Earth to learn the lessons we set forth in our plan and we are destined to repeat those exact classes until they are mastered. The scenery and the teachers may change, but the lesson remains. Eastern religions have often interpreted karma to mean that whatever we put out will come back to us manyfold, but they rarely further explain that devious actions only come back to us when they are done maliciously. We often get caught up in our belief systems and forget that the divine knows what is truly in our hearts and minds. Remember the elementary school teacher with the sole ambition of protecting the children? Our true intentions are paramount. As mentioned before, societal law is generally concerned with our actions only, but the universal law is focused on our intentions.

Not only do we pre-plan the goal of our existence, but, once we are here, we use our free will to make choices that bring either more positivity or more negativity into our world. When you choose the behavior, you also choose the consequence. Life is a series of choices. "One's philosophy is not best expressed in words; it is expressed in the choices one makes...and the choices we make are ultimately our responsibility," endorsed former first lady Eleanor Roosevelt. We do not live by chance, but by choice. Through our choices, we create our own karma. Every act touches a cord somewhere in the universe and life responds accordingly, reciprocally to the frequency we emit. Therefore, there is no one to blame, except ourselves, for the status of our lives. The physical plane provides us with opportunities to make choices and learn lessons that would not be possible without a physical existence, without physical needs, wants and desires.

In the East, Buddha's answer to our question of suffering is that we experience suffering solely through our attachments to worldly wishes. This suffering is caused by our own desire for life to be different. In the West, we commonly ask questions like, "Why does God allow such evil to exist?" and "Why is there so much suffering in our world?" God is not the source of our suffering. God does not create the negativity in our lives, we do. "Everything in the world – the desire of the flesh and the desire of the eyes and the showy display of one's means of life – does not originate with the Father, but originates with the world," 1 John 2:16. Life is about experience, nothing more, nothing less. We suffer at our own hands. We create our own unwarranted fears. We create our own illusions. We label people and we judge their behavior. We create negativity through our thoughts, our choices and our actions. We create negativity from our own reluctance to separate from our worldly possessions and we create negativity from our unwillingness to take responsibility for our own actions. God is not to blame.

"The blame is his who chooses: God is blameless."

PLATO

One of the objectives of this book is to help you understand that there is no longer a need to ask the questions, "What did I do to deserve this?" or "Why am I being punished?" Karma is not retribution; it is more of a return on your investment. We have all heard the saying, "You reap what you sow," which is the modern version of the Bible verse, Galatians 6:7. The concept of karma supports the expression, as does the law of attraction. Every act has a consequence. If we put out positive thoughts and actions, the consequences will be positive. If we put out negative thoughts and actions, the consequences will be negative. Most people consider karma to be about good balancing evil. Karma does not mean that if we are gifted one apple, one apple will be stolen from us; rather, it means that if we give away one apple, something equivalent to that apple will be returned to us, oftentimes manyfold. It is a balancing of actions; however, it is a balance of good for good and bad for bad, not good for evil. Thus, the removal of all negative karma becomes the ultimate goal for our souls.

The following quote from Robert Ingersoll, former American political leader, sums up the concept of karma beautifully, "Happiness is not a reward, it is a consequence. Suffering is not a punishment, it is a result." Karma ultimately honors integrity and deals with futility, however, it is not a judgment system inflicted on us by a higher source. God is love and only love; He does not punish nor judge. One of the most recited Bible verses, Matthew 7:1, is, "Judge not, that ye be not judged," and ironically, one of the major causes of our world's negativity is judgment. Some systems of belief, still today, rely heavily on a fear of judgment by imposing rules that do nothing but judge behavior. These doctrines judge not only the behavior of their own congregation, but also the behavior of believers in other philosophies, deeming them not suitable to enter paradise. They insist that a decisive punishment will come on some sort of ultimate judgment day, once a person's spirit leaves their physical body. For those of us that truly believe the Higher Source is nothing but love, it is extremely difficult to understand how the idea of an all-loving Creator came to be based on fear, guilt and exclusion. This reliance on fear is the leading reason the perception of hell has become so enormously embellished.

The concept of an eternal torturous place of pain was used by the church during the dark ages to scare people into the pews and into obedience. Interestingly enough, the Bible does not have that much to say about hell; consequently, the details came from our poets, not from our prophets. Aurelius Augustinus, a Romanized Berber philosopher and theologian of the fourth century, later canonized as St. Augustine, spent his early days in a drunken state. As he grew, he began to develop remorse for his squandered youth and set out to find true meaning in his life. He wrote, "I reasoned for as far as I could go and I still couldn't make the jump to religious belief." This frustration sent him into a state of madness. His mother, while on her death bed, convinced Aurelius to convert to Christianity and from this, he began to devise and distribute strict policies on salvation and damnation. He played a critical role in creating regulations against lustful acts and sexual behavior. This power made him very pessimistic toward women and sex and quickly his dark message found a ready audience. Holy men latched onto his teachings and used them to further their own agendas. These teachings provided a means, without using force, to convince people to follow their word. Hell soon became more and more real in a time saturated with disease, famine and war. It was an easy transition into believing there was an equally cruel afterlife. Patrons would fill the church to listen to the gruesome stories of pain and torture. It was like attending a weekly horror film. Hell became the spectacle, the attraction itself. And, in a time of small towns and rare travel, what was taught in the church was taken for absolute truth. The churches were also filled with art and architecture that depicted evil creatures and this possible place of torment, so, patrons would not only hear the sermon and feel the power of the word, but they were also surrounded aesthetically with reinforcements. The suggestion of an actual personified ruler of this place, the devil, developed from this same artwork as it became increasingly more elaborate, with each artist attempting to outdo the other.

The concept of hell has snowballed over thousands of years and traveled through endless translations, but there is no hell as we so frequently identify. Those that choose to read the religious scriptures literally believe hell is a physical place, though, when we genuinely think about it, would an all-loving being permanently banish one of his own creations? Would He abandon them in their utmost time of need? Would He leave them to suffer for all of eternity? On the other hand, your mind might jump to the question of duality, that if there is rightly a paradise, there must also be an opposite position, correct? Well, we must first remember, duality only exists in the physical plane, not in the spiritual plane, which is the sole reason we take human form, to learn in an environment that allows for this duality. Therefore, there would be no need for such a place of eternal torment.

"There is no death. How can there be death if everything is part of the Godhead? The soul never dies and the body is never really alive."

Isaac Bashevis Singer

In the spirit world, there are no punishments for wrong behaviors and no rewards for right behaviors. The knowledge gained through our earthly experiences moves us along the evolutionary ladder toward perfection of the soul. These experiences are not meant to lead to some form of judgment or punishment. Once we return to our spirit form, we humbly evaluate our recent progress and then decide what it is we need to include during our next trip. In the physical world, there are only choices. No good choices, nor bad choices, simply choices. We are here to simply "experience", yet, we undergo so much self-imposed suffering from this perpetual threat of judgment. This threat is the primary reason most people agonize over why God would allow such suffering to happen in the first place. It is through suffering that our soul learns and becomes perfected. Suffering has a noble purpose, the evolution of our soul. Our struggles are merely disguised opportunities to grow. Through adversity we are introduced to our true selves, not only our weaknesses, but also our strengths.

Now, when we re-visit the question, "What did I do to deserve this?" we should have a clearer understanding of how to interpret our own situations. The idea of *deserving* something easily takes on a negative connotation, as if the consequence of your action is some sort of payback. When, in reality, the outcome is more *earned* than deserved. If you put out good, you get good in return. If you put out chaos, you get chaos in return. If you put out heartbreak, you get heartbreak in return. The result may not always return in the same costume, the same flavor or even the same year, but the equivalent will eventually appear and the settling of karma will never escape you.

The second question of, "Why am I being punished?" often comes from someone that does not realize their own internal power. They are not consciously aware that their own actions will show up later in life and that each of their decisions helps shape their very future. When faced with any choice, we must always stop and contemplate the future outcome of that choice, not only the immediate benefits, but also how this particular choice will turn up down the road. Like a piggy bank that holds your fortune, great consideration should be paid to the positive karma level in your karmic bank and every effort should be made to continuously add to that level. Also, even though something feels like a punishment, it may not be so. Remember the story of the farmer and his horse? His quality of life continued to improve, despite the neighbors' reactions.

The quality of each of our lives is completely in our own hands and is relevant to the choices we make daily. Everything we do is a step toward something else. Each little decision, choice or action affects the world. Thus, we should all pay a little more attention to how our actions affect, not only ourselves, but also those around us. We can never really be sure how far the impact of our actions will travel, so a safe route to take would be to simply "be nice for everyone else's sake". Each one of us has an ongoing internal struggle and when we are feeling low, we tend to forget about others and become a bit self-involved. We all owe it to our co-workers, our friends, our partners and our families to be as kind and pleasant as possible. Studies show that a person's social network affects their mood and that we are constantly affected by the emotional state of everyone around us, thus happiness is basically contagious and we each play a vital role in the happiness level of everyone we encounter. Simply being nice is a selfless act that takes the focus off of you and places it onto others, which will inevitably lighten the load for all of mankind.

Frequently, people place blame outside of themselves simply because they do not understand the relationship between what is currently happening in their lives and their overall hopes and dreams. In this world, there are sufferers and learners. The meaning derived from each of our experiences is open for personal interpretation, yet this interpretation dramatically affects our quality of life. Although the challenging times may be necessary, misery is optional and martyrdom is a choice. There is always a quiet wind gently pushing each of us further down this spiritual road. We will all move forward eventually, either willingly or reluctantly. We can choose to drive life or we can allow it to drive us. We can choose to live in our own heaven on Earth, or our own hell on Earth. To utilize one's own power and steer life, is heaven. To never become aware of our own power is to drift, and hell is to drift. We would save ourselves a lot of undue worry if we would only accept the so-called sorrows for what they are, mere experiences, and then have the patience and trust to wait for the end of the story. Once you are able to recognize these sorrows as such, you will learn to appreciate the growing pains just as much as their counterparts and this is a true sign of wisdom. Shifting your focus and having goals and aspirations that you are moving toward, rather than problems and conflicts that you are moving away from, is much more productive for personal development. Albert Einstein once said, "In the middle of difficulty, lies opportunity." Real learning takes place in the heat of every challenge and this is where we develop the most confidence and faith in our own hidden power. Personal power and inner freedom come from understanding the purpose of our "suffering", instead of losing ourselves in it. But, does this mean we have to go through life wearing rose-colored glasses? No, but it does suggest that we should be just as thankful that thorns have roses as we are that roses have thorns.

Despite all of this, does it seem that sometimes you receive more than your fair share of difficulty? That karma has it out for you personally? That pain and sorrow have you on speed dial? Well, keep this is mind: there are over six billion people on this planet. Does it seem logical that the divine would be picking on you independently? When put in that context, it does not seem rational, does it? Consider this, of those six billion people there are also six billion charts in action. They are all different, each and every one of them. We need every level of the spectrum; otherwise, we would all be the same. Imagine if we were the same, or even similar. The world can only handle so many rock stars, or so many politicians, or so many religious leaders. We are all living our chart beautifully and it takes each of us to make the world function. Therefore, we should all appreciate each individual path just as they were written. We may all be on varying soul levels, but let's not forget that we are all working toward the same goal of perfection. Our gift to the world is not to judge, but to observe and learn. There is a well-known quote that describes the beauty of our individuality and purpose, "I am just as my Creator made me, and since He is satisfied, so am I." No two women, nor two men, are exactly alike and there is something very magical about this phenomenon.

During the pre-birth planning stage, we choose the life we want to live and how much past-life karma we intend to meet and settle. Souls often seek to heal in later lives the aspects that were left unhealed in previous lives. This is a form of divine justice with the goal being to become so enlightened that all of our negative karma has been settled and we no longer need to reincarnate to take on more karma and suffering. Life challenges are written into our charts, often as a method of slowing us down so we will take the time to acknowledge the beauty surrounding us. We also write challenges into our chart for the purpose of serving others. The Dalai Lama, or, "the compassionate one", was once quoted, "My religion is kindness." He describes a spiritual life as an ethical life, a life devoted to the service of others. Our charts were designed with others in mind. We work with, not only our spirit guides, but also others in our soul group to establish a plan that will provide opportunities to meet each of our goals. Our soul group includes those at the same evolutionary stage with whom we have shared lifetimes, possibly playing the role of husband, wife, daughter, son, brother, sister, mother, father, friend or enemy. Because we are part of these soul groups, we oftentimes discover that other humans seem familiar to us before we even meet them and that some human bonds are instantaneous and unusually strong. This familiarity sometimes appears through the phenomenon of déjà vu and may be attributed to residual cell memory from past lives. Members of the soul group often play specific roles for each other during the earthly experience, thus ensuring the desired challenges will surface. In this way, your friend is your need answered. The pain and suffering we decide on collectively is by choice and in the name of service. The problem with these choices often surfaces when we get to Earth, where we realize we were a bit overzealous in the planning and the weight of our selected challenges begins to overwhelm us.

Human existence definitely requires a significant amount of courage, a word which comes from the Latin word <u>cor</u>, meaning "heart". Some souls exhibit incredible courage and select the highest form of human sacrifice, the sacrifice of earthly body. This occurs when one plans to experience a form of disability or deformity in order to take on pain so others may live life free of this pain. This chosen life theme is Fallibility, in which they set an inspiring example for the rest of the world and the restrictions of their physical limits often help create unrestricted patterns of thinking. This choice may have also occurred in order to allow others to learn to love unconditionally or to resolve ego-driven issues. Members of this group often bring out the very best in every person they meet and they shine among the brightest stars and should be valued as such as they serve as constant reminders to live a life filled with gratitude. Others choose to experience a lack of what they most want to understand and appreciate, as in the concept of duality. Until we understand one polarity, we will never fully understand the other. It is the absence of something that best teaches its value, i.e., love. Living without love in our lives often finds us continually striving to get it from any possible direction, whether it is the right kind of love or not. Challenges are remarkable mirrors that reflect our feelings about ourselves and our world. We simply meet another version of ourselves every day. If we have body images, we often are faced with situations that require us to deal with those images. If we struggle with impatience, we are often faced with situations that require us to exhibit patience. Thus, these challenges may be construed as gifts. Knowledge and awareness helps us recognize them as such and wisdom allows us to appreciate them and apply an appropriate meaning to them.

The idea of suffering creates fear and anxiety. Anxiety is typically anchored either in the past or in the future, rarely in the present. Whenever you focus on the present, you generally find that it is actually satisfactory. Conversely, "When you worry about the problems of tomorrow, you are creating unhappiness for yourself today," declared Shantidasa, Buddhist scholar. Anxiety encourages us to think about past regrets or future worries, and, although thinking about the past does help us understand the patterns we are repeating, living in the moment alleviates the fear of the unknown, the future. There is great freedom in living your life without fear of the unknown. The unknown currently has nearly seven million Americans affected by Generalized Anxiety Disorder. That is an alarming amount of individuals that are struggling with living in the moment. A Course in Miracles states that there are only two basic human emotions, love and fear, and that they cannot co-exist in one space. In the same manner, doubt and fear cannot occupy the same space as hope and action. Feelings of peace, joy and elation indicate we are acting and thinking in ways that are consistent with our true nature as loving souls. Feelings such as doubt and fear suggest we are not. We must all take action in our own lives. We must each become a student of life and shed the label of victim. As students, there are lessons that we teach and lessons that we learn in every single encounter. Each time we are drawn to Earth to face our challenges we grow a little bit stronger and a little bit wiser. We also grow in confidence, as did Antaeus, the giant wrestler in Greek mythology. His mother was Gaia, the Goddess of Earth. She was the source of Antaeus' strength. Each time his opponent threw him down to Earth, he gained more courage to stand up and fight. His defeats made him stronger, virtually rendering him unbeatable. The human experience is quite the same, we grow stronger each time we are thrown to Earth and we eventually become undeterred by the thwarts of our opponents.

We may consider those same opponents to be our enemies, the people that tend to cause us stress or those that often complicate matters, but, not so. They are our teachers, sent for us specifically. The Dalai Lama clarifies, "Without enemies, you could not learn patience and tolerance, therefore, the enemy is the real teacher." We should strive to appreciate our enemies in the same way we appreciate our challenges. As your wisdom grows, gratitude will become your only reaction to each and every situation. Increased wisdom will allow you to become thankful for every trouble and to consider them a true blessing. The saying "a blessing in disguise" no longer applies to a person with spiritual wisdom. Their blessings are no longer under disguise and no longer go undetected. They understand that we are generally given whatever it is that we are, not necessarily whatever it is that we believe we want.

"We have two lives: the one we learn with
and the life we live after that."

Bernard Malamud

The Native Americans have a spiritual tradition of teaching everything in circles or wheels. They have long shared their Sacred Hoop, or medicine wheel, that originated from these traditions. This wheel represents the sacred circle of life, but a new perspective on this wheel is the "mistakes wheel" which details the essence of learning. The five areas of the wheel symbolize the various types of "mistakes" we make as humans. Although we know that nothing we do is truly a mistake, rather simply a choice that was made, the same principle may be applied to the concept that everything we encounter is a teacher. The wheel is sectioned into four quadrants that each extend out of a smaller center circle. In the north quadrant is the learning that we gain from our own mistakes. The east quadrant includes the learning we gather from the mistakes of our teachers and our teachers are all around us, every single moment of the day. The south quadrant contains the willingness to make as many mistakes as it takes to gain knowledge and the west quadrant houses the learning we acquire from the mistakes of others. And, to chime in with the teacher philosophy, the center circle emphatically states that there is no such thing as a mistake. Through this example, we can clearly see that our own earthly education comes from every angle. Everything speaks. We learn, not only from our selves, but also from everyone and everything around us.

Native American Mistakes Wheel

☆ (center) Learning that there is no such thing as a mistake

Chapter 5

The Gift of Suffering

"May all that have life be delivered from suffering."

GAUTAMA BUDDHA

Suffering may seem inevitable in this physical plane; nonetheless, there are many different forms of suffering. The self-imposed suffering we endure from our worldly attachments and the suffering we see through destructive behaviors, painful experiences and debilitating diseases are just a few examples of the heartbreaking pain we see in our world. The way we respond to this suffering varies greatly. There are those that wallow in their own pity and never attempt to understand the reason behind their hardships and there are those that continually seek out knowledge to help them understand the ways of the world.

We all have the ability to see opportunity where others may see problems, yet few take the time to reflect and grow. Just as there are countless potential causes for wounds, there are also countless ways to respond to each situation and begin to heal those wounds. It is always how you choose to react that determines the impact. Your chosen attitude is a monumental choice. Your mind-set may turn out to be a driving force or a severe disability. Every single move you make in this world is based on a choice, even the most mundane tasks, such as picking up your child's coat or doing a load of laundry.

These are choices, conscious or unconscious, nonetheless, choices. Empower yourself with the phrase, "I have a choice right now." Use this phrase whenever you are facing a personal challenge. Focusing on a positive response will create a more constructive energy, which in turn will increase your level of awareness and understanding, eventually leading to complete gratitude.

Take the child's coat for instance, before you bend down to pick it up you may be thinking about how many times you have picked it up before or how many times you have given them the speech about looking after their own things. But, instead of being upset about their actions, you decide to switch your thoughts to the power of your own choice. You then decide to pick up the coat because you know how much your child loves the coat and how it would upset them to see it ruined. You have positively shifted your thoughts from potential resentment to an attitude of service. This choice is not about their lack of anything, but about your chosen response to the situation. Your own choices will either alleviate your suffering or create it; meanwhile, the child is oblivious to your thoughts or actions. However, this example by no means indicates that you should not teach your child how to look after themselves, it is only a reminder that you are in control of your own emotional well-being.

Your choice of attitude is crucial in how you live your life, but undoubtedly just as important is what you feed your mind. We must always be conscious of the messages we are sending to our subconscious minds, even through the music we listen to, the movies we watch and the people with whom we associate. These messages are your mode of transportation through life. They create your life. By focusing on the positive, your mind will shift its attention and it will begin to see things differently.

I have been known to encourage others to stop "why-ing". Instead of continually asking the question "why?", change the question to "what?" What was the reason behind this encounter? What was the lesson designed specifically for me? What role did I play in the outcome? Asking the question why? involves being a victim. Asking the question what? involves an empowering search for an understanding, an attempt to find a solution, an attempt to problem solve. Personal awareness is key in initially recognizing the reaction and then action must take place to change the behavior. You must first catch yourself reacting negatively and then you will be able to take steps toward positive change.

Our own actions play a significant role in our overall attitude and we must begin to use each experience as a growth opportunity. Our society is built on judgment, for reasons of creed and reasons of vanity. Knowing that we each designed our path for the greater good, there really is no need to judge ourselves or others for our perceived "mistakes". As we have learned, there are no mistakes, only choices, and we shall never pity anyone for their choices. To pity someone means to see them as a victim and no one on Earth is a victim. We are each merely following our pre-determined path. Instead, we should train ourselves to empathize, appreciate and learn from them. We may never fully understand the path of another, nevertheless, we must respect their eternal wishes and remind ourselves that they may be having the exact experience they desired. Whenever I am having a difficult time understanding a situation, I contemplate what the person may be seeking to learn or contribute, rather than how traumatic it may all seem at the moment. Sometimes I am able to make sense of their wishes, other times I am not. However, it is not my position to judge their circumstances. It is merely my position to value their contribution to all of mankind. We must also realize that if we cross paths with someone, they are there to assist in our growth as well as their own. Each encounter has a dual effect and each individual involved has an opportunity for growth. With awareness, we can use this knowledge to work toward our own perfection.

We are often scarred from our childhoods, the same childhoods we carefully selected because we knew they would provide the exact circumstances necessary to overcome our karmic debt or to learn the lessons we most desired to learn. This hypothetical scarring hits us most in the heart, where we develop our capacity to love. We emerge from childhood with scars from insufficient parenting, excessive pampering, extreme extravagance and feelings of failure. As children, we often suppressed our own needs in order to fit into the mold of society and many of us endured devastating physical and emotional abuse from those expected to protect us. The list of damages is infinite, yet it is this very damage that stimulates our growth the greatest. In the words of Helen Keller, American author, "Character cannot be developed in ease and quiet. Only through experiences of trial and suffering can the soul be strengthened, vision cleared, ambition inspired and success achieved." If it were not for the scars we endure, we might live our lives fully content without ever questioning anyone or anything and thus, we would miss out on the path of self-discovery.

"We are not held back by the love we didn't receive in the past, but by the love we're not extending in the present."

Marianne Williamson

Childhood experiences often encourage us to become protective of our hearts, leaving us to forever struggle to open them up to others or to new experiences. This struggle may seem like a disadvantage in the timeline of life, however, without this struggle, lessons of love would never be pursued and the ultimate lesson in each of our lives is the development of the capacity to love. This is the lesson behind all lessons, learning to love unconditionally, without judgment or fear, and using that love to live a life of service. However, our wounds keep us from venturing beyond the safety of our habits, our routines, or our homes. We avoid situations that may require us to think outside the box. We long for that sameness, that familiarity, that comfort. The same comfort discussed earlier in Buddha's Second Noble Truth, the truth of the cause of suffering.

Some wounds make us vulnerable. We fail to realize that we have rights, the right to protect ourselves, the right to choose for ourselves and the right to stand up for ourselves. We feel unworthy of our successes and find it difficult to say no to others, even against our own judgment, for fear of disappointing someone else. Our charts are written with these precise scars so we may first experience them and then learn to overcome them. Experience is the most effective teacher. For example, a profoundly benevolent soul with the desire to deepen her level of compassion may choose to incarnate into a highly dysfunctional family. Since the absence of something is often the best teacher, in this case, the lack of compassion in her outer world forces her to turn inward, where she rediscovers her own compassion.

A thorough review of your own childhood may lead to new discoveries. Evaluate what you were able to acquire from your childhood challenges and determine where you would be today without those skills. Would you still be the strong, independent woman you are today if you had not experienced a less than compassionate father or a single, hard-working mother? Would you still be the ever-present father for your own children if you had not experienced distant, often cold, parents during your childhood? Would you still be the intellectual force you are today if you had been the athlete you longed to be and spent your early years with a ball rather than a book? Conversely, would you still have those same leadership skills or that enhanced level of self-discipline if you were not that skilled athlete during your formative years? These are acquired traits, but what about the skills you learned from coping with an alcoholic sibling, an abusive parent or a less-than-kind stepparent? Remember, these scenarios were a direct request from you and, despite the neglect we see in the world today, there really is no such thing as bad parenting. They were simply doing the best they knew how to do at the time. When we know better, we do better. As difficult as it is to admit, they were playing their role perfectly for those around them and the best we can do is to help each other discover our lessons and find our own personal power. In retrospect, how many times have you thought to yourself, or heard someone else say, "It was the best thing that ever happened to me." Or, "If that had not happened in my life, I would not be the person I am today." Our adversities spring us forward by forcing us to face our desired challenges. They provide us with a chance to come back even stronger. Hypothetically, if I were to ask a room full of people to write down their current troubles on a piece of paper, wad them up and throw them into a pile, most would have little difficulty with this task. If I were to then ask them to pick one paper out of the pile with the option of trading troubles with another, most would pick their own paper, because that is what they are equipped to handle. Our experiences make us who we are and, if given the choice, most would not want to change.

Each detail of your life has had purpose. Examining these details without placing blame will give you a better understanding of your own path. No one is to blame for anything that happened in your past. There is, in fact, no blame at all. There are only lessons, lessons learned or lessons overlooked. There is no blame, no judgment and no punishment. The universe does not punish us by making bad things happen, karma is an impersonal law. If we slip and fall, we do not blame gravity or feel victimized or punished by it. The same goes with karma, it is not retribution; it gives equivalent to what we give. It is a reciprocal relationship, but one in which we hold the reins. Courageous Souls, written by Robert Schwartz, beautifully details the pre-birth planning sessions of ten individuals who worked with gifted mediums and channels to discover why they chose their greatest life challenges. These narratives include some of the most agonizing obstacles, involving physical illnesses, physical handicaps, drug addiction, alcoholism, the death of loved ones and random accidents. These recounts help us understand that even the most painful situations move us forward. For example, a poverty theme may mean that you learn to overcome it by not succumbing to it or that you may be balancing karma from another lifetime where you stole riches from another. A person that takes on a caretaker role may feel burdened by the need to care for another person when the challenge may have been specifically selected in order to overcome self-centeredness or to settle debt from the abuse of their own body during a past life. An accident may be nature's way of getting your attention if you travel off track, a method of getting you to take stock of your own life. Otherwise, you may never slow down long enough to even notice what is happening around you and, how does one learn life lessons without even noticing their life? Personal growth is possible not only for the person involved in the accident, but also for all those surrounding that person. Each encounter or experience we have is designed for our own benefit, so we must take notice and seek out the lesson.

Group karma occurs when members of a soul group plan an incident in which they experience together for a certain purpose, such as natural disasters that take out entire cities or populations, or events such as the Holocaust, or diseases like HIV/AIDS. These major events tend to get all the "glory", but honestly we suffer more at our own hands than we do from these catastrophes. Yet, under the concept of dualism, as tough as it may be to contemplate, there is always a positive side, more 'story' on the way, even in the most abysmal times. The 2010 earthquake in Port-au-Prince, Haiti was undeniably devastating. Consequently, when something like this happens, we immediately want to know why; yet, it was easy to see how it opened the eyes of the world and woke us up to the heartache and the overwhelming need to pay attention. It served as a harsh reminder to all of mankind and when necessary attention gets paid to something, help generally follows. In this case, the world responded with an outpouring of love, compassion and support, all of which are helping raise the vibrational frequency of the planet. This is not to dilute or downplay the existence of these human lives, in fact, it is quite the opposite. It gives reason to celebrate their chosen willingness and sacrifice and honor the lives that were given for the betterment of humanity. These volunteers likely agreed pre-birth that if the frequency of the planet was not at a certain level by such a date, they would volunteer to participate in something that would help raise it to the desired level. Acts such as these take into consideration the big picture, the world view, not just the individual experiences, but the overall experience of humankind. Because of these sacrifices, despite the gloom we often feel, the frequency of our planet continues to rise. Look at our race over time. There is more compassion in our world today than ever before in our history. We are growing more aware of each other and of our habitat daily and our choices and our outreach reflect that awareness. Thus, these willing individuals are essentially helping heal humanity. Every step of the way they are teaching tolerance, compassion and love. The trials and tribulations we experience on Earth are so insignificant to the joys we will experience on The Other Side. Our souls can never be destroyed and they will continue to exist beyond our human lives, thus, it is likely that these individuals are already peacefully at work developing a new plan for their next earthly trip.

The earthquake in Haiti was a horrific natural disaster, but what about the causes, such as the Holocaust, that promote suffering from acts of intolerance, segregation and supremacy? In order for these causes to take place, there must also be individuals that become the voice of the movement, for example, terrorists. Ironically, terrorists are victims too. They are victims of the illusions and stories they have been told. Yet, great evil can create great good. On one hand, Adolf Hitler appeared to be a sadistic, evil monger, but from a different perspective there is a component of hidden heroism. If he had won the war, he may just have been considered the greatest ruler of all time by his followers. There were people during his time that considered him a hero, just like many other historic leaders, i.e., Napoleon Bonaparte and Julius Caesar. Take our own country for instance, the United States of America, any president that calls for war will be regarded as a hero by some and a villain by others. It all relies on your personal perspective.

Hitler once preached, "We must create the new man so that our race will not succumb to the phenomenon of degeneration so typical of modern times." He believed that by weeding out the biologically inferior, those draining valuable resources, that he was actually benefitting civilization by driving evolution forward and creating a better humanity. He was only thinking economically and essentially he was de-valuing human life. His actions make it challenging to understand his contribution to the world. Perhaps Hitler's pre-birth plan was to serve as a Persecutor, an aggressive self-satisfying sociopath who would abuse or even kill without guilt or remorse, or perhaps he was to serve as a Victimizer, chasing absolute control over as many victims as possible for the purpose of being surrounded at all times by visible proof of this power. Whatever the case, his voice reigned supreme in Germany for twelve years before he eventually committed suicide in order to avoid humiliation at the hands of the Soviet troops. The Third Reich basically collapsed after his death, along with many of his ideals, and his existence served to warn the world against the dangers of following a false prophet. Again, even unthinkable acts shed a light on the injustices in the world and eventually propel us forward.

As always, and just as importantly, there is the concept of duality and an opposite position for these acts. The other volunteers involved in these causes may have chosen the life theme of Follower, Pawn, or Victim, to name a few. Followers are just as essential to society as the leaders, since one does not exist without the other. What the Follower has to keep in mind at all times is the importance of carefully selecting who and what to follow. Pawns, which are also essential in the advancement of the universal spirit, use their role to ignite something of great significance, be it positive or negative. They must also be vigilant in choosing which causes to support. Victims are our sacrificial lambs and their sacrifices bring to light injustices and inspire others to make changes for the better. Victims include abused and murdered children, targets of hate crimes and others wrongfully accused of felonies.

"The highest result of education is tolerance."

HELEN KELLER

Intolerance is one, if not *the* biggest, offense. With love and compassion being the utmost goal, intolerance is the furthest away from that objective. It keeps us from loving others and appreciating each other's uniqueness and contribution to the whole. The beggar on the street teaches tolerance. The HIV/AIDS sufferer teaches compassion. The addict down the street teaches acceptance. We have the desire to change everything based on our own expectations or our own comfort levels, but we should be careful not to impose our expectations onto others. Quite possibly the homeless person on the street has no intention of changing their circumstances. We must learn to live and let live. This is not to suggest that we should ignore those in need, but that we should be careful not to judge them and that we should use the experience as a personal reminder to live with empathy and to extend gratitude. When we do, we exemplify tolerance and compassion and this emotional strength will bring each of us, and those around us, peace and joy.

We will each continue to encounter our pre-planned challenges until we face them. Until then, they will circle around us like hunters after their prey. Thus, it may seem that suffering is inevitable, but life is not just one long insufferable journey. We must all tackle our charts and the challenges written within, but we must also look at the entirety of our lives, not only the imperfections. The quality of our journey is determined by how quickly we discover our lessons and learn to overcome them. This can always be accomplished with love. Even if we never completely understand the lessons before us, actions of love will unfailingly lead us down the path toward perfection. Love and kindness break all barriers. No matter which path you follow, if it is paved with love, you will never be lost.

"Out beyond ideas of wrong-doing and right-doing there is a field. I'll meet you there."

RUMI

We commonly lose our way because of the sting of judgment. The words and actions of others often construct our highest hurdles. God does not judge and neither should mankind. Although we are often our own worst critic, we should never judge ourselves because we are each a part of God and therefore we would be judging Him. The concept that God, an all-loving being, judges has confused theologians for centuries. If He were to practice judgment, that would humanize Him, yet so many religious beliefs are based on judgment, not love. In the final words of German poet Heinrich Heine, "God will pardon me, that's his line of work."

Judgment is useless because it separates us from those we judge. It creates exclusivity and attempts to place us on a higher plane than others and that is just not accurate. We are all creations of the same source. We are all fighting our own battles on the path toward perfection. No one person is working harder or faster than any other person. We are each traveling our own paths at the pace we are capable of traveling. We must be willing to honor the path of others because, no matter how much we want to interject, staring at a newly planted seed will not make it grow any faster. Judgments only create fear and prevent us from remembering that we are all one. Our most harsh judgments often fall on those facing the most difficult charts and, rather than condemn them, we should be giving thanks for their act of selflessness. Granted, their gesture of love may have been selected to balance selfishness from the past, but the past and their karmic debt is not our concern. We should only be concerned with the gift of the present and how each encounter spurs our own growth. Keep in mind that any resistance to our paths, or any resistance created in the lives of others, makes the trip that much more complicated. One of Deepak Chopra's Seven Spiritual Laws of Success is The Law of Least Effort. This law asks for us to simply accept people, circumstances and events as they occur and to take responsibility for our own situations. So, rather than fighting life, we should respond with love. Whenever we act with love, the world surrounds us with the same.

"Whatever I fight weakens me.
What I cooperate with strengthens me."

68TH VERSE, TAO

Challenges are inevitable and the people we choose to surround ourselves with are crucial to our success. The company you keep will greatly determine the trouble you meet, so it is important to be selective of those you allow into your intimate life. With that in mind, it is true, there are dark entities in this physical plane. They are misguided souls that were created just as you and I were, in the likeness of God, yet they chose to separate themselves from God utilizing their own free will, just as the allegory goes about the angel Lucifer. In the beginning, God created the angels, including Lucifer, and then he created man. God asked that the angels serve man as their protectors and guides and Lucifer, unwilling to honor or serve anyone over his ultimate love, the Creator, refused to serve man. This refusal alienated him from God, which is the theoretical meaning of hell, "a separation from God". Those that choose to separate from God are allowed to continually exist on Earth so that we can learn in a plane that contains negativity and evil. Without their negativity, we would not have duality, therefore, no place to acquire the knowledge we so desperately seek.

Giving meaning to our suffering is vital to our growth. We should all strive to handle each challenge in a manner that will help us grow. Questioning whether an incident was good or bad is irrelevant. The intent is to gain valuable personal growth from each and every experience and when we miss the lesson we are acting with ignorance, an unknowing. We are acting without awareness. Therefore, it is this ignorance, not sin, that creates the mental and physical suffering. The world God created is perfect, just as He planned. Jesus said, "In this world, you will have tribulation; but be of good cheer, I have overcome the world," John 16:33. Another version reads, "I have told you these things, so that in me you may have perfect peace and confidence. In the world you will have tribulation and trials and distress and frustration, but be of good cheer. Take courage; be confident, certain, undaunted! For I have overcome the world. I have deprived it of power to harm and have conquered it for you." The divine is not concerned with our physical bodies. Our souls are of greater importance to Him than anything earth-bound. Even when we are stricken with diseases that impair the body, the divine remains focused on our spirit and uses the illness to encourage further movement along our spiritual path toward perfection.

"It is not the physical body that should worry us. Rather, our concern must be to live while we're alive- to release our inner selves from the spiritual death that comes with living behind a façade designed to conform to external definitions of how and what we are."

Elisabeth Kubler-Ross

We all experience pain, but do you sometimes experience suffering from your envy of others? Do you often feel that your life is not as grand as it is supposed to be? There is an old Yiddish saying, "One always thinks others are happy." Our consumer society creates comparing minds in humans. We are constantly sizing up those around us, often leading to feelings of inadequacy, destroying the joy we could be experiencing. Peace is eternally available to us and we do not need to do anything more than change our own thoughts. The outside environment or how others think and act is immaterial. We must be conscious of who and what we are comparing ourselves to each day. Let's say that you currently earn $75,000 per year in a job that you no longer enjoy. Do you find that your loss of enjoyment stems from the fact that you are constantly comparing yourself to a friend that makes over $100,000 and that you find yourself coveting the things her money can buy? Have you wondered if she compares herself to others and, if so, to whom? She is most likely comparing herself to those making $500,000 and they, in turn, are likely comparing themselves to those making over $1,000,000. Everyone is comparing themselves upwardly, thus creating self-imposed feelings of inadequacy. Compared to a large majority of the population, you are making a very desirable salary at $75,000. When you compare yourself to this population, you may enjoy increased levels of confidence and pride in your accomplishments, thus renewing the enjoyment you receive from your current position. Scientists call this a "downward comparison," which is remarkably effective at boosting happiness. One comparison makes you miserable and the other comparison makes you happy. One brings you suffering, the other brings you joy. The choice is yours. The choice is always yours.

We are conditioned by society and we develop expectations based on that conditioning. We create unnecessary suffering through these expectations, as well as through our attachments to the world. Imagine how the expectations of a young woman that has her mind set on receiving a well-scripted, grandeur marriage proposal, complete with a magnificent jewel, from her longtime boyfriend would create needless trouble for her if he instead chose to propose in a more informal, personal manner using a family heirloom. Her own expectations may end up letting her down because his actions did not reflect her expectations. His love for her was no less grand than before, yet her pre-determined ideas separated her from enjoying the moment and celebrating the love they share. She may have cheated herself out of enjoying the moment, based solely on her expectations. Another example of how our expectations rob the joy from our experiences occurs through our established customs, such as holiday traditions. We set ourselves up for failure by expecting an event to go a certain way and if it does not go exactly as planned, we find it difficult to see past the infraction and simply enjoy the event. Whereas, if we became a little more flexible and relished the moment more, the event would work itself out and provide enjoyment for all.

Our fears are often based, not in reality, but on our expectations and our angst about those expectations. Many share the fear of running out of time, the fear of not getting married at a certain age, the fear of not having babies at a certain age, the fear of wanting to buy a house by a certain age, etc. These fears are anxiety driven and unfounded. Change your expectations and your world will change. If you expect to have a life void of challenges, you are misinformed. If you acknowledge and accept your challenges for what they are and learn from them, you will enjoy peace. "When we surrender, we allow the universe to work its magic; we say yes to infinite possibilities; we trust that things will work out as they are meant to; and we give our self permission to let go of the outcome. This can be liberating, intimidating, blissful, scary, and a swirl of so many other emotions. But in the end, if we are true to our heart, life unfolds with magnificence…and we get to celebrate," acknowledges Davidji, dean of Chopra Center University. You have within you that type of power and the sooner you realize it and use it to your advantage, the sooner you will enjoy a life full of joyfulness and serenity.

Attempts to control what is uncontrollable or neglecting what is within your own power often leads to sorrow. We should all shift our focus to the person we want to become, rather than on the expectations imposed on us through the external world. My younger self used to be concerned with what others thought of me. Today,

I am mostly concerned with what I think of me and there is great pride and peacefulness in being able to say that I am the person I aspired to be. This strength inspires me to help others find their own happiness and live a life of true authenticity.

"It takes courage to grow up and turn out to be who you really are."

E.E. Cummings

Spending time thinking about the direction we are headed is vital, yet, we rarely take the time to *think* at all. We have on average over 60,000 thoughts per day, so what are we contemplating during those moments? The very word "man" comes from the ancient Sanskrit word which means "to think" and the term "Homo sapiens" is Latin for "wise man" or "knowing man". Rene Descartes, French philosopher, said, "I think, therefore I am." Man is supposed to be a thinking being, yet we live in a hurry-up society where we spend, on average, nearly seven hours "plugged in" each day. The ongoing debate between science and religion has been going strong for centuries and, despite all of the technological advancements during that time, man rarely takes time to reflect on his own existence. Albert Einstein chimed, "The splitting of the atom changed everything, except for the way man thinks." Instead, we are overloaded with information and caught up in the busy-ness of life, which rarely converts to a lot of time spent on reflection. Have you ever really thought about how you spend your time? Our time is more precious than gold, yet we spend it so frivolously. There are 1,440 minutes in one day and 10,080 minutes in one week. These moments turn into how we live our lives. How many of those precious minutes do you spend reflecting on your own personal journey? One in every four persons reads zero books per year, yep, zero. With that being said, the major concern here is where then are we getting all of the information that is clouding our brains? In the western world, we spend great chunks of time engaged in mind-numbing activities, activities designed to simply occupy our mind and make us *not* think. In the eastern world, reflection and meditation are predominant and claim a large part of the daily philosophy.

"All men's miseries derive from not being able to sit in a quiet room alone."

BLAISE PASCAL

Spending time alone is crucial to our personal growth, though this is a daunting thought for the majority. First, many feel like it is a selfish act to put themselves before others. When, in reality, spending time rejuvenating your spirit and getting to know yourself better only deepens your levels of understanding, tolerance, patience and compassion. These are all traits that any friend or family member would benefit from and should desire in another. Second, finding time for solitude in our busy lives can be quite difficult today and last, but not least, few people are actually comfortable spending time alone. Many are actually frightened by the thought. I am amazed, yet not surprised, at the number of people I have encountered that need constant entertainment in one form or another. Silence is golden and can do wonders for the psyche. When we decide to take real time to separate ourselves from the world, we find out who we really are inside and this discovery leads to enlightenment.

"Make time for quiet moments, as God whispers and the world is loud."

ANONYMOUS

Chapter 6

Understanding the Self

"When you hear about the Self, meditate upon the Self, and finally realize the Self, you come to understand everything in life."

Brihadaranyaka Upanishad 4.5

In order to understand human life and find our way to enlightenment, we must first know our Self. Maya Angelou, American poet, once said, "No man can know where he is going unless he knows exactly where he has been and exactly how he arrived at his present place." This statement strengthens the above Hindu saying about the Self and reaffirms what we have already discussed about how understanding the challenges in our lives will lead to personal acceptance, growth and fulfillment. But, if the Self is truly our starting and ending point, then exactly what is the Self? And, how do we get to know the Self?

The evolution of the collective soul remains the overall objective and that evolution depends upon each individual transcending ego. This means that first we must each uncover our authentic self. Every choice that we face is a choice between love and fear, a choice between listening to our heart, or listening to our ego. We are each divinely created with an intact ego that wears glasses that only allow an external view. The ego keeps us tied to the world and is wrong-mindedness, which is based in fear. We must remove these glasses and see the world and ourselves from an internal perspective. Here lives our soul, a place of right-mindedness, which is based in love. Love is the ultimate goal and the highest frequency to which we may aspire. Love is the peak expression of compassion and tolerance. Love is the most powerful emotion, but it is not only a feeling, love is also an ability, something we do, something we embody. Love is a choice, love is a decision.

"Love bears all things, believes all things,
hopes all things, endures all things."

1 CORINTHIANS 13:7

A human being who has reached a higher level of consciousness and who has come to know the true concept of reality is able to apply their spiritual knowledge to the conduct of their life and that is spiritual evolution. Through the application of this knowledge, the awakening of dormant, or sleeping, capabilities is achieved, often considered an "awakening". The belief is that the average human is only partially conscious and, as a result, most are considered to be asleep to reality. This ordinary human condition, this waking sleep, comes in part from ancient spiritual teachings, such as those of the Buddha. The word Buddha itself means "one who has achieved bodhi". Bodhi can be translated as "awakening" or "enlightenment".

The traditional definition of enlightenment refers to coming to the end of the developmental process, or to "have arrived". In the evolutionary framework, enlightenment is not about coming to the end of anything, but rather to the beginning of something else. We were all created with this innate power; therefore, I tend to believe that there are not necessarily enlightened beings, but more so, enlightened behavior. As humans, we have this mysterious impulse to evolve, to be connected, yet, we are already evolved, we are already connected, some of us are just not yet living consciously aware and thus are not exhibiting enlightened conduct. You as a soul are immortal. There is only the process of being who you have always been. The evolution of consciousness is simply the awakening process. Consciousness simply means awareness, the awareness of one's true existence.

Awareness involves becoming conscious of the intention that has been operating in your life. "Intention is the starting point of every spiritual path. It is the force that fulfills all our needs, whether for money, relationships, spiritual awakening, or love. Intention generates all the activities in the universe. Everything that we can see – and even the things we cannot – are an expression of intention's infinite organizing power," Deepak Chopra. Far too often we believe that we have no choice about how our lives are unfolding, but when we become aware of our intentions and take responsibility for our choices, the truth of our path becomes explicit. This leads to spiritual evolution and maturity. If immaturity is the inability to use one's own understanding without guidance from another, then spiritual maturity involves leading a courageous, conscious life, an awakened life, an enlightened life, in accordance with one's own understanding. The motto of enlightenment, as set forth by Immanuel Kant in his 1784 essay, Answering the Question: What is Enlightenment?, is: "Sapere aude! Dare to be wise! Have courage to use your own understanding."

"Knowing others is intelligence; knowing yourself is true wisdom. Mastering others is strength; mastering yourself is power."

TAO TE CHING

The majority of us go through life as complete strangers to ourselves and thus we live our lives according to how society dictates. Instead, we must spend time exploring our innermost thoughts and feelings and opening ourselves up to the divine. "Everyone thinks of changing the world, but no one thinks of changing himself," expressed Leo Tolstoy, Russian novelist. Genuine confidence comes from knowing and accepting yourself, including your strengths and your limitations, rather than relying on acceptance from others. A lack of self-confidence often comes from trying to be someone you are not. This struggle between accepting ourselves and pleasing others creates resistance and this resistance creates emotional suffering. A Chinese proverb states, "Tension is who you think you should be. Relaxation is who you are." When you are able to be your true self, you no longer have competition. You will no longer be fighting the personal war inside your own head. "Then you will know the truth, and the truth will set you free," John 8:32. Once you accept yourself just the way you are, you will no longer have any judgments about yourself. And then, once you accept yourself, you will be able to accept everyone else just the way they are without judgment. You are no longer in conflict with yourself and you are no longer in conflict with anyone else. Having no judgment creates silence in the mind. Mother Teresa once responded to concerns of acceptance in this manner, "Life is not a competition. The relationship is between you and God, not you and everyone else." In this context, our only concern should be our connection with the divine. Another beautiful statement from a NDE survivor in the book, Evidence of the Afterlife, reads, "I discovered that I had personally chosen to take on a physical body and have the life experiences I was having. I realized I had wasted time in suffering, and what I should have been doing was using my freedom to choose true love, and not pain, in all that came into my life." This realization highlights the effect of our daily choices and how they essentially create our lives. Simply by deciding to choose love, over pain, you will be able to rid yourself of unnecessary suffering.

"The most difficult matter is not so much
to change the world as yourself."

Nelson Mandela

The beginning of enlightenment is to first know yourself. A person does not need to attend church or a synagogue to find themselves; they only need to find time for solitude, reflection and introspection. The Self is not out there somewhere to be found, it is internal and always with us. If I were to ask you to identify yourself with three words, you would most likely throw out nouns, such as mother, teacher, lawyer, words that only represent your external life. When, in actuality, we should acknowledge our inner-being foremost and that would require adjectives, such as kind, patient, loving. I am kind. I am patient. I am loving. This is the essence of who you are. Pope Gregory I advised, "Be not anxious about what you have, but about what you are." When we consider our contribution to the whole, what becomes more significant, the size of our home or the number of people we welcome into it? The title on the office door or the manner in which we treat our fellow workers? The number of clothes in our closet or the number of people we help to clothe? The neighborhood we live in or how we treat our neighbors?

Introspection will lead us to new discoveries. Our conscience, the counselor within, is always guiding us toward perfection. It nudges us through our intuition and assists us in distinguishing the quality of our acts. The voice of your mind is very loud, but your conscience is constantly whispering to your mind to do the right thing. Most of the time we get confused by our mind, or the ego. It does not accept our oneness with the world, it searches to separate and to be considered special. It pushes us toward familiar ground, in the direction of our habits and our comfort zones and we often oblige because we have become definite creatures of comfort. Instead, we must learn to listen to our conscience. These gentle whisperings come during moments of calmness, quiet and awareness and lead us to discovering our inner splendor. This is why the Om mantra is used during many meditations or chants. It is not so much a word, but rather an intonation, which transcends the barriers of race, age and culture. It is believed to be the basic sound of the universe and to contain all other sounds. It puts us in touch with that central vibration or energy that is the universe. The sound resonates through the body and penetrates to the center of one's being, the soul. Listening to your conscience allows you to gain control over your mind. Gaining control of your mind and allowing your soul to light your path is an early hurdle on the path to illumination. This control allows you to work toward awareness and toward living a fully conscious life.

"There is no illness of the body apart from the mind."

SOCRATES

We can create many diseases with our mind and we can heal ourselves with this same mind. The Course in Miracles sees all human ills as rooted in mental illness and all solutions as lying in mental healing. As we heal ourselves, we also heal the world. Yet, the soul needs no improvement, it is already perfect. Only the mind needs to change. This is all the more apparent in our current age of discovery. Our body of knowledge is rapidly growing, yet we are not responsible for creating this body of knowledge. We are merely seeing it with more aware eyes and gaining insight into what has always been. Ralph Waldo Emerson agreed when he said, "People only see what they are prepared to see." This naivety may be necessary because only when the pupil is ready, will the teacher appear.

"The real voyage of discovery consists not in seeking new landscapes, but in having new eyes."

MARCEL PROUST

Through silence, through journaling, through practices such as meditation and prayer, you can explore who you are. This exploration will lead to both awareness and mindfulness. Mindfulness can be translated as the ability to pay attention to your life, including your feelings and your actions. In order to reach this awareness, you must pay complete attention to all of the things you do during your waking hours, which can prove to be extremely difficult in this world full of distractions. A Canadian friend of mine once told the following story and it quickly resonated with me because it acknowledges how often we put our focus on immaterial things and leave the truly big things to mere chance. The story begins with a reunion at a prestigious university, where a group of graduates were gathered. Their former professors were delighted to see them again and hear about their life successes. Shortly into the gathering, the graduates were offered coffee. One professor went into the kitchen and brought out two large carafes of coffee and a tray of cups. The cups were of the mixed variety, some were bright, some were bland, a few were large, a few were small, some were chipped and some were oddly shaped. The group politely, yet swiftly, proceeded to help themselves. Once everyone was holding a full cup in their hand, one of the wise professors asked, "Did anyone notice how quickly we all rushed to take the more stylish, lavish cups first, leaving the others behind? Yet, we freely poured coffee from either carafe without a second thought?" The group stood in puzzlement. It is normal human behavior to want the best for ourselves, but this skewed focus often becomes the source of our stresses. What the graduates were really after was the coffee, not the cup, yet they all rushed for the cups, without being concerned about the coffee. Life is like the coffee, what we are all chasing, and it is the real gift. The positions in life, the high paying jobs, the prestige, the honors, the glory in society, those are all cups. They are merely tools to hold and sustain life. The quality of the coffee does not depend on the cup. If you only concentrate on the cup, you never really enjoy or even taste the coffee. Choose to enjoy the coffee and worry little about the cup. However, in this day and age, when coffeehouses are on every corner and we are able to special order our drinks a dozen different ways, the story seems a bit implausible. The point though is that we spend so much time concerned with outer beauty, rather than on getting to know or understand our inner beauty. We tend to dwell on material possessions and forget about the inner substance.

"People travel to wonder at the height of mountains, at the huge waves of the sea, at the long courses of rivers, at the vast compass of the ocean, at the circular motion of the stars; and they pass themselves without wondering."

Saint Augustine

We are very lucky as Americans living in the free world. We have so many choices of how to live our lives. We also are free from the overbearing censorship that other countries endure. China has ongoing censors on what gets in, i.e., internet searches are highly guarded in regards to the Dalai Lama. Their leaders are convinced that he seeks to destroy China's sovereignty by pushing independence for Tibet. When, in fact, the Dalai Lama unshakably stands for non-violence, unity and world peace. Most consider him to be the divine incarnation of Buddha, as well as Head of State. For us in the west, it would be like Jesus Christ incarnated and sitting in the White House. Such is the power and significance of the Dalai Lama to his people. Yet, an entire country is unable to benefit from his wisdom because of an unfounded fear of anarchy. In 1959, Chairman Mao said to the Dalai Lama, "Religion is poison and undermines the progress of any country." He was obviously concerned that religion might divide the loyalties of the public.

Fortunately, in the United States, we are free to believe as we wish. Our beliefs are not dictated by our government. Still, we are restricted in many ways. Following visits to our country, the Dalai Lama observed that other countries seem much richer than America, despite our wealth. He commented on our apparent greed and our limitless desires. He accredited these as the source of our problems and the source of our suffering. We always want more and we are never satisfied. He has said, "The happiest people are often the poorest," yet, amusingly, we pity them. These people have very little to worry about because they have very little. This is a true testament to the power of living a simple life. Only when we have a lot, do we feel like we have a lot to lose. "Poverty consists in feeling poor," wrote Ralph Waldo Emerson, American author. Even the very affluent experience anxiety from the multitude of choices they face. Fewer choices often equals fewer desires and less anxiety over whether the choice made was actually the right one. For the less fortunate, there are fewer decisions to be made and they can generally be found content. This contentment is important. Life can be extremely hard in these places, yet crime is low. There, they experience endless patience. Here, we have so much, yet, because of our expectations, we are often quick to anger, jealousy and deceit.

In the wake of Buddha, the Dalai Lama teaches tolerance and compassion. Political and religious leaders of the world must remain focused on the same virtues; instead, they are often swayed by money and power. However, in order to live with the same sense of compassion, understanding and tolerance that the Buddha talked about, they must remain open and tolerant, yet most are not. All of the creeds of the world have the potential to create harmony and peace of mind. They all basically stand for the same thought, yet they disagree because they have different names for their deity. Perhaps the focus should be more on the message, rather than on the messenger. The Dalai Lama insists on peaceful solutions and he allows no violent acts in his name. What if all world leaders exhibited this same fortitude? Maybe we would all put down our weapons and strategize peacefully. Mother Teresa rejected attempts to have her join any marches against violence, but instead she quipped, "When you hold a march *for* peace, I'll be there."

Over two-hundred years ago, in 1792, Dr. Benjamin Rush, founding father and signer of the Declaration of Independence, proposed an Office of Peace that would equal the efforts set forth for the Department of War. This agency would work for world peace and promote creative ways to avoid conflict. Intriguingly, the United States has had an established Department of War since 1789, three years before Rush's proposal, yet no Department of Peace has yet to be fully established. We currently have a Department of State that promotes America's interests overseas and a Department of Defense that fights for these interests, however, it is apparent that there is a fear that a department focused on peace may interfere with these economic affairs, threatening the overall power of our country and the survival of America as it is known.

I have often wondered what would change if we were able to read the auras of our political and religious leaders. True intentions would be on display and may create some significant changes in the world. Any war or conflict creates mutual suffering and no one wins. Therefore, it is in everyone's best interest to promote peace and love.

It may not seem probable at the international level, but we can each promote it in our own little worlds. "Never doubt that a small group of thoughtful, committed citizens can change the world; indeed, it's the only thing that ever has," advised Margaret Mead, American anthropologist. Lead by example. Be an instrument of peace. In the words of Mahatma Gandhi, "Be the change you want to see in the world." In whatever ways you can, create peace. It is extremely difficult to argue with someone that is not obsessed with winning, or being right. "Conflict cannot survive without your participation," Dr. Wayne Dyer, American author and self-help advocate. Apply love. Always choose love over pain.

With all of our creative freedom, our total body of knowledge is said to have doubled between 1900 and 1950 and then again between 1950 and 1958 and now it is said to be doubling every five years. Nonetheless, even with this incredible increase in knowledge, and our freedom of choice, only 45% of Americans are satisfied with, or even like, their current job and more than one half of Americans with jobs are actually dissatisfied with them according to a recent report by The Conference Board. This is the lowest approval percentage in the 22 years of the report. Today, we rarely pursue careers based on our passions or our innate talents. We are enticed by money and power and greed. We are willing to make these types of sacrifices in order to accumulate more *stuff*; essentially, we sell our souls, all the while creating more suffering for ourselves. These positions often come with built-in competition so everyone involved is constantly stressed by the threat of failure or the threat of job loss. Then, when we finally get home from work, we are not interested in putting out any more effort or using any more brain power. We choose to engage in activities designed to keep us from thinking. We watch reality shows to escape our own lives, we search for security through our electronic connections, cell phones, internet, etc. and all of these actions inadvertently limit our ability to actually interact. We no longer are as aware of our immediate surroundings. These instruments keep us attached to the world, to our egos, to the constant security of having others accept us and validate us. "Technology is a way of organizing the universe so that man doesn't have to experience it," Max Frisch, Swiss novelist. Personally, I would love to see just as many faces stuck in a book as there are stuck in these electronic devices, or at least be able to see faces looking at other faces. I have always believed in moderation, because it is the extremes that lead to problematic issues. It is so easy to lose the mind-body connection in this quick fix society. We need to be able to be alone, to connect to nature, to the divine and to our thoughts. We must spend time leaving the world behind and getting honest with ourselves. Knowledge is power and the knowledge of how your own mind works and what your soul desires is the most beautiful and productive knowledge of all.

"Thinking: the talking of the soul with itself."

Plato

Only when the clamor of the outside world is silenced will you be able to hear the deeper vibration that is your soul. Reflect. Think. Accept yourself. Accept others. Forgive yourself. Forgive others. Evaluate, accept and appreciate the past. Enjoy, learn from and value the present. Anticipate, create and invite the future. This quality time with your Self is just as important, if not more so, than physical exercise is for the function of your body. The brain is equipped to change in response to learning; it is essentially a learning machine. Simply by thinking a little, we can change our physiology significantly. By replacing the negative with the positive, we can change our entire lives. "If we understood the power of our thoughts, we would guard them more closely. If we understood the awesome power of our words, we would prefer silence to almost anything negative. In our thoughts and words we create our own weaknesses and our own strengths. Our limitations and joys begin in our hearts. We can always replace negative with positive," states Betty J. Eadie in her heartwarming book, Embraced by the Light, written about her own near-death experience.

"We only think when we are confronted with problems."

JOHN DEWEY

Any dilemma forces us to think in order to problem solve. Our moments of "suffering" force us to stop and contemplate. This thinking leads to awareness. This awareness leads to conscious living, which in turn leads us to our life's purpose. We often think of death as the ultimate enemy, when it is actually our thoughts. "If you realized how powerful your thoughts are, you would never think a negative thought," advised Peace Pilgrim. Reflection helps us become more familiar with who we are and, in order to make any change, we must first know our starting point. We must first understand that we have a need for change, a sickness of sort. Once we realize this need, we can set about fixing or healing that sickness. One has to first realize the illness before the healing may begin, for without this knowledge, there would be no desire to find a cure or make a change. Once you recognize that you are suffering, once that revelation has been made, naturally you will try to find out what lead to that condition. You will then wish to be free from that illness and you will be willing to apply all possible medications and explore all possible treatments. Spiritual wisdom may be obtained from understanding the origin of our illness and true happiness may be attained once we possess this wisdom.

"Happiness is something that you are and
it comes from the way you think."

DR. WAYNE DYER

Ignorance is a state of suffering from not understanding that we are sick. The antidote to ignorance is wisdom. "Science is organized knowledge. Wisdom is organized life," Immanuel Kant. Wisdom is achieved by practicing mindfulness. Mindfulness is achieved through practices that free our mind from our own thoughts, including past experiences and future anticipations. We must investigate ourselves through these practices, this introspection, and find our own truth.

Even Jesus Christ, the apostle of love, spoke not of conforming, but of transforming. "Be not conformed to this world, but be ye transformed by the renewing of your mind," Romans 12:2. His method of "saving" us was to teach us, so we would know what to do on our own. He did not recite a myriad of rules or regulations. He did not force his will upon us. He was not asking for submission. His message was merely one of peace and love. He taught us to be kind, to live without judgment and to love unconditionally. He needed no temple, nor any elaborate rituals. His teachings were simple and direct. The common thread of compassion that rings through all of his teachings also rings true for most other world religions. "So in everything, do to others what you would have them do to you, for this sums up the Law and the Prophets," Matthew 7:12. This simplistic Golden Rule, or Ethic of Reciprocity, may be found in nearly every ancient writing or religious text, including Buddhism, Confucianism, Hinduism, Islam, Judaism, Sufism, Sikhism and Taoism. It seems it would have been sufficient for this to be the only commandment because they all build from this idea. This simple philosophy rises above all of the varied costumes and rituals and maintains that our sole focus should be on how we treat our fellow man. This is the true meaning of life, to live without judgment, to live in peace and to love unconditionally. "Love thy neighbor, as thyself," Matthew 22:39. Everything else fades away once we find that type of peace and we then delight in our own life of gratitude.

"True religion is real living; living with all one's soul, with all one's goodness and righteousness."

Albert Einstein

Chapter 7

Accepting the Assignment

So, where do we go from here? Accepting the assignment to live your life with purpose and to live out your chart ultimately begins with personal awareness. Once you have personal awareness, you are then able to be a model of compassion for the world to follow. Honesty is crucial. You must be honest with yourself during this journey of self-discovery. Mindfulness leads to awareness and requires that we actually pay attention to what life is offering us in each moment of our lives. This mental state demands that we free our mind from our own thoughts, including those of our past and of our future. We have to be willing to devote time to our Self and to the pursuit of the truth. We have to want to make a change. We have to have the courage to take personal inventory of ourselves and our daily choices, as well as the effects of those choices.

If taking this hard look at yourself seems daunting, another way to accomplish this same goal is to begin the search by helping others. This route shifts the focus away from your needs and eventually reveals the status of your inner being. If, on the other hand, you are prepared to look at yourself, then go for it. Start within. Find what ails you and apply all possible medications. If you are against racism and there is even one ounce of it in your own heart, start there. If you are opposed to intolerance and there is even a speck of it in your own heart, start there. If you cringe at the thought of cruelty, yet you make choices that show cruelty toward others, start there. Consider what it is like to be your friend, your co-worker, your neighbor or even your partner. Are you generous with your love? "If you have only one smile in you, give it to the people you love. Don't be surly at home, then go out in the street and start grinning 'Good morning' at total strangers," Maya Angelou. First begin at home, then take it outside. Mentally trade places with others. Walk a mile in their shoes. Imagine living with their battles. Replace anger with kindness. Replace fear with curiosity. Replace indifference with compassion. Understanding your own tendencies, emotions, and true character will help you begin to feel compassion toward the whole world, both nature and mankind, and this will change your life. Aeschylus, Greek playwright, wrote, "Character is fate." The manner in which you act toward the world, it will respond. Apply love. Be a guiding light. Exhibit the change you wish to see, for the only way to master love is to practice love.

"Stop what you are doing long enough to grow."

JOHN C. MAXWELL

Savor moments of silence and solitude. "You cannot be lonely if you like the person you're alone with," Dr. Wayne Dyer. Appreciate yourself. Appreciate your surroundings. Extend gratitude for everything in your life and if you are not able to find gratefulness for something, learn to let it be and trust that eventually the reason will reveal itself to you. Be patient with yourself. Listen to yourself. Journals are a magnificent way to be heard without talking. Begin a gratitude journal to remind you of your joys and your successes. Spend time each day acknowledging, and writing down, at least three things you did well that day, or three things you did that brought peace to the world.

Become a good finder. Search for the good in other people and in every situation. "I cried because I had no shoes until I saw a man who had no feet," Russian proverb. Put your life in perspective. If I were to ask you to fill up two suitcases, one with the good things in your life and the other with all of your troubles, which one would fill up faster? Appreciate your life. Find at least three moments of the day to be thankful. For me, when I first began this journey I focused on the following three moments of each day: immediately upon waking up each morning, the moment when I reached for the doorknob of my home after being away and again as I laid down to sleep at night. Eventually, these small acts of awareness turned into a constant stream of appreciation.

Studies have shown big leaps in the happiness and energy levels of those who take good care of themselves and who are grateful for their blessings. Grateful people are typically less attached to material possessions, seeing them as fleeting and appreciating the time actually spent with the item, rather than taking it for granted. They are also less likely to be envious and more willing to share their blessings with others. Being grateful is often about paying attention to whatever is right at any given moment. This does not mean they are oblivious to the world. They are simply aware that even though everything may not seem ideal, there is a universal magic working its wonder at all times. This awareness leads to good thoughts and good feelings follow good thoughts. Therefore, acknowledge what is right and speak positively about yourself and your life in order to create these good thoughts. Good feelings will follow and they will fill your life with joy.

"God does not simply will that we should be happy,
but rather that we should make ourselves happy."

IMMANUEL KANT

Once this appreciation becomes daily practice for you, observe what you have surrounded yourself with, from the people in your life, to the objects in your house. Detachment is one of the toughest hurdles for those of us in this consumer society. Yet, in order to grow, you must learn to detach from material possessions and from the expectations of the physical world. "The wise man carries his possessions with him," Bias. You must make sure everything around you is current with the person you are today. Clutter weighs on our minds and shields us from the world. Keeping emotions tied up in our attachments is detrimental to our progress. If something in your possession is no longer congruent with the person you are now, it is actually doing you a disservice. The item is limiting your closure, your release and your advancement. The actual experience of clearing out clutter is often therapeutic and provides undeniable relief. However, although it may seem difficult to let go of certain material possessions, they are often easier to release than our attachments to others. We use our attachments to other people in order to validate ourselves. This is one of the glaring reasons many find it difficult to be alone, because in those moments they are forced to validate themselves. If we are to truly live our charts and live for ourselves, we must draw strength from our own convictions and be solid in the fact that we are acting out of love, compassion and oneness with the universe. If our intentions are honorable and our actions match, the rest is immaterial. If you purchase a gift and you are certain it is perfect for someone, generally you are extremely anxious to watch them open the package. But, is this excitement based on their enjoyment or your own pride in having purchased the gift? Their reaction should have little to do with the actual act of giving. If the act was done out of complete love, their reaction would not matter. When we scrutinize their reaction looking for validation, it leads to our own self-doubt, our own feelings of inadequacy and of feeling underappreciated. Or, it inflates us with self-importance and arrogance, all tools of the ego. This creates suffering. The attachment to their validation creates suffering that could have been avoided if we would have detached. You will never be able to control or even understand another person completely. The way to enlightenment is to focus on your own soul and allow everyone else to do the same.

While you journey toward enlightenment, it is important that the people in your life support your ideals and your growth. Surrounding ourselves with others that bring us joy will allow our hearts and minds to remain open and positive. Being torn between your own desires and the desires of those around you can significantly hinder your efforts. "If the mind is scattered, it is powerless," Dalai Lama. Continually strive to think good thoughts. It is impossible to feel bad and have good thoughts at the same time. Your self-worth comes from actually thinking and believing that you are worthy. Only the insecure continually seek out security. Typically, those who pursue the most approval, receive the least, and those who pursue approval the least, receive the most. We must learn to let go of, not only our prejudices and our judgments, but also our expectations and our need for approval. We must learn to let it all go. Our happiness should not depend upon someone else. We create our own happiness through our thoughts and our actions.

We must detach from our need for others to approve of us and from our unrelenting impulses to hold resentment toward others. Forgiveness will lighten your own load and conversely, it will lighten the load for all of humanity. We must also detach from our need to control others. Unconditional love, true compassion, exists in the willingness to let those around you be exactly who and what they want to be, without any contention that they gratify you. Remember, they are playing their role beautifully and that benefits all of mankind, no matter your level of understanding of the situation. You must also forgive yourself for any regrets you may have from the past. Holding on to these feelings only impairs you in the present. Consider that you did something ten years ago that you regret and still to this day you punish yourself for that choice. You are still suffering from that past experience, and not because the event is still happening, but because you are still holding it in your mind as if it is still happening. This is what the Buddha meant by fleeting moments. Everything is simply an experience. You must let go to move forward. If any of your thoughts or actions are weighing heavily on your mind, they will obstruct your ability to concentrate and without the ability to think clearly, there will be little or no progress made toward personal insight. We must have compassion of self first. Compassion is the divine expression of love and having compassion for ourselves, and forgiving ourselves, helps us move forward and identify with others that are also suffering.

Understanding suffering allows us to act empathetically, first toward ourselves, and then toward others.

We should always aim to have complete harmony of our every thought, word and action. Always aim to purify your thoughts because a mind at peace is stronger than any universal force. Once your mind is at peace and you begin to understand your own self-worth, you will understand the importance of each moment of your life. "Until you value yourself, you won't value your time. Until you value your time, you will not do anything with it," M. Scott Peck, American author. Do you find yourself wishing it was Friday, on Tuesday? That is wishing your life away. Be mindful. Live with more intention. Create the life you want to live. It's not about finding that one big answer to the meaning of your life; rather, it's about finding meaning in every single moment of your life. A true sign of wisdom is the ability to see the miraculous in the seemingly ordinary.

Use your valuable time to pursue wisdom, to learn. We lose energy when life becomes tedious. Our minds get bored easily and need to be continuously stretched and when we stretch our minds, we stretch our hearts. Get interested in something outside your norm. Lose yourself in a new passion. "The more you lose yourself in something bigger than yourself, the more energy you will have," Norman Vincent Peale, American author. The act of lifelong learning allows our hearts to grow a little bit each time we are exposed to new ideas, new cultures, or new philosophies. When our hearts are open, we learn to appreciate differences and notice similarities. We learn to live and let live. We learn to *just be.* Nevertheless, learning to *just be* is much more difficult than it sounds. Learning to *just be* involves acknowledging the value of everything in the universe, not only a fraction of it, but the entire universe. "There are no extra pieces in the universe. Everyone is here because he or she has a place to fill, and every piece must fit itself into the big jigsaw puzzle," Deepak Chopra.

Break down your fears. Overcome them with knowledge and awareness. Only when we are no longer afraid, do we truly begin to live. Live a full life guided by the Golden Rule, a rule so simple, yet so overlooked; a rule so straightforward, yet so forgotten.

Whichever way you choose to say it, the Native American way (the Great Law of Peace), "Respect for all life is the foundation," or the Islamic version, "None of you truly believes until he wishes for his brother what he wishes for himself," or the Hindu variation, "This is the sum of duty: do not do to others what would cause pain if done to you," the principle is clear, albeit the application is hard. Imagine if everyone woke up one day and resolved to live by this one rudimentary rule. The world would be a much different place. Begin here. Embody tolerance. Spread compassion. Send a message of peace and acceptance wherever you go. Lead by example. Be a role model for the world. Carry with you always an open heart and an open mind. Live in harmony with yourself, with those around you and with the universe. It is a choice and the choice is always yours.

"To live is the rarest thing in the world.
Most people exist, that is all."

Oscar Wilde

Chapter 8

The Invitation

The following poem was included simply as an extension of the preceding chapters. It beautifully describes the concepts in this book, but under the guise of a wise soul looking for its counterpart. My own heart broadens with every read and I wish the same for you. Enjoy.

<u>The Invitation</u>

It doesn't interest me what you do for a living. I
want to know what you ache for and if you dare
to dream of meeting your heart's longing.

It doesn't interest me how old you are. I want to
know if you will risk looking a fool for love, for
your dreams, for the adventure of being alive.

It doesn't interest me what planets are squaring your moon.
I want to know if you have touched the center of your
sorrow, if you have been opened by life's betrayals or have
become shriveled and closed from fear of further pain.

I want to know if you can sit with pain, mine or your
own, without moving to hide it or fade it or fix it.

I want to know if you can be with joy, mine or your
own, if you can dance with wildness and let the
ecstasy fill you to the tips of your fingers and toes
without cautioning us to be careful, to be realistic,
to remember the limitations of being human.

It doesn't interest me if the story you are telling me
is true. I want to know if you can disappoint another
to be true to yourself; if you can bear the accusation
of betrayal and not betray your own soul, if you
can be faithless and therefore be trustworthy.

I want to know if you can see beauty, even
when it's not pretty, everyday, and if you can
source your own life from its presence.

I want to know if you can live with failure, yours
and mine, and still stand on the edge of a lake and
shout to the silver of the full moon – "yes!"

It doesn't interest me to know where you live or how much
money you have. I want to know if you can get up, after
the night of grief and despair, weary and bruised to the
bone, and do what needs to be done to feed the children.

It doesn't interest me who you know or how you came
to be here. I want to know if you will stand in the
center of the fire with me and not shrink back.

It doesn't interest me where or what or with whom
you have studied. I want to know what sustains
you, from the inside, when all else falls away.

I want to know if you can be alone with yourself and if you
truly like the company you keep in the empty moments.

Oriah Mountain Dreamer, Indian Elder

Additional Quotes

The secret of health for both mind and body is not to mourn for the past, worry about the future, or anticipate troubles, but to live in the present moment wisely and earnestly.

Buddha

One man gives freely, yet grows all the richer, another withholds what he should give, and only suffers want.

Proverbs 11:24

You become the pinnacle of success as soon as you become uninterested in money, compliments, or publicity.

O.A. Battista

The highest form of ignorance is when you reject something you don't know anything about.

Dr. Wayne Dyer

There are things known and there are things unknown, and in between are the doors of perception.

Aldous Huxley

Perception is a mirror, not a fact. And what I look on is my state of mind, reflected outward.

A Course in Miracles

A man should look for what is, and not what he thinks should be.

Albert Einstein

For the man who prays in his heart, the whole world is a church.

Sylvain of Athos

What each of us learns has the potential of becoming a message to all humankind.

Barry Neil Kaufman

Be a lamp, a lifeboat or a ladder.

Rumi

Happiness doesn't depend upon who you are or what you have. It depends solely on what you think.

Dale Carnegie

Fear less, hope more; whine less, breathe more; talk less, say more; hate less, love more; and all good things are yours.

Swedish Proverb

If when you look into your own heart, you find nothing wrong there, what is there to fear?

Confucius

There are only two tragedies in this life: one is not to get what you want and the other is to get what you want.

Oscar Wilde

Real difficulties can be overcome; it is only imaginary ones that are unconquerable.

Theodore N. Vail

Burdens become light when cheerfully borne.

Ovid

A small trouble is like a pebble. Hold it too close to your eye and it fills the whole world and puts everything out of focus. Hold it at a proper distance and it can be examined and properly classified. Throw it at your feet and it can be seen in its true setting, just one more tiny bump on the pathway of life.

Celia Luce

Do all the good you can, by all the means you can, in all the ways you can, in all the places you can, at all the times you can, to all the people you can, as long as ever you can.

Reverend John Wesley

Just a Few of the Books that Have Illuminated My Path

A Course in Miracles - Helen Schucman/Foundation for Inner Peace

A New Earth: Awakening to Your Life's Purpose by Eckhart Tolle

Change Your Thoughts-Change Your Life: Living the Wisdom of the Tao by Wayne W. Dyer

Courageous Souls: Do We Plan Our Life Challenges Before Birth by Robert Schwartz

Destiny of Souls: New Case Studies of Life Between Lives by Michael Newton, Ph.D.

Embraced by the Light by Betty J. Eadie

Evidence of the Afterlife: The Science of Near-Death Experiences by Jeffrey Long, MD with Paul Perry

Life After Life by Raymond Moody

Life After Death: The Burden of Proof by Deepak Chopra

Many Lives, Many Masters: The True Story of a Prominent Psychiatrist, His Young Patient, and the Past-Life Therapy that Changed Their Lives by Brian Weiss

Same Soul, Many Bodies: Discover the Healing Power of Future Lives Through Progression Therapy by Brian Weiss

Science and the Akashic Field, An Integral Theory of Everything by Ervin Laszlo

The Alchemist by Paulo Coelho

The Four Agreements: A Practical Guide to Personal Freedom, A Toltec Wisdom Book by don Miguel Ruiz

The Fifth Agreement: A Practical Guide to Self-Mastery by don Miguel Ruiz, don Jose Ruiz and Janet Mills

The History of Hell by Alice K. Turner

The Light Beyond by Raymond Moody

The Other Side and Back by Sylvia Browne and Lindsay Harrison

The Power of Intention by Wayne W. Dyer

The Power of Now: A Guide to Spiritual Enlightenment by Eckhart Tolle

There is a River: The Story of Edgar Cayce by Thomas Sugrue

The Secret by Rhonda Byrne

The Power by Rhonda Byrne

The Seven Spiritual Laws of Success: A Practical Guide to the Fulfillment of Your Dreams by Deepak Chopra

"Be always at war with your vices, at peace with your neighbors, and let each new year find you a better man."

Benjamin Franklin